D0112035

KenteCloth

KenteCloth

Southwest Voices of the African Diaspora

The Oral Tradition Comes to the Page

Edited by Jas. Mardis

University of North Texas Press
Denton, Texas

ity of North Texas Press

Printed in the United States of America
First edition

5 4 3 2 1

The paper in this book meets the minimum requirements of the
American National Standard for Permanence of Paper for Printed
Library Materials, Z39.48.1984.

Permissions
University of North Texas Press
PO Box 311336
Denton TX 76203-1336
940-565-2142

Library of Congress Cataloging-in-Publication Data

KenteCloth : southwest voices of the African diaspora / edited by
Jas. Mardis.
p.   cm.
ISBN 1-57441-047-4 (cloth) . –ISBN 1-57441-040-7 (pbk.)
1. Afro-americans—Southwestern States—Literary collections. 2. Afro-
Americans—Southwest, New—Literary collections. 3. American
literature—Afro-American authors. 4. American literature—Southwestern
States. 5. Southwestern States—Literary collections. 6. Southwest, New—
Literary collections. I. Mardis, Jas., 1961–   .
PS566.K46   1998
810.8'0896079—dc21
97-44983
CIP

Cover design by Good Eye Design
Cover art is from the series "The Ancestors and the Womb"
by Annette Lawrence

CONTENTS

PERFORMERS

TELLERS

SIGNIFIERS

Acknowledgments

I would like to acknowledge the support and promotional efforts from everyone throughout the region who continues to say "Yes" to writers. Those same people—in the bookstores, coffee shops, churches, schools, homes and other venues that support these unpublished writers—have kept alive the very important writing that makes this collection possible. As well, I will be forever indebted to the clerical contributions of Ms. Etta Riles and Mr. Colson Jacnal, without whom many of these manuscripts would have been subjected to my heinous typing efforts. These volunteers offered their services out of the same dedication and appreciation as bookstore and coffee shop owners. As well, their editorial insights were very helpful in keeping me focused on the task at hand. Everyone who heard about this project recognized and accepted its importance. I hope that such recognition will continue, and make *KenteCloth: Southwest Voices of the African Diaspora*, a canonical contribution to the literary landscape.

Clifton Taulbert's "The End of a Season" is from *When We Were Colored*, 1989 (Council Oaks Books); 1995 Penguin Books.

James Mardis's "Sting" is from *New Texas 94: Poetry and Fiction* (Center for Texas Studies).

Ife Mahdi's "One Friday Nite at Boone's Adult Club" is from *One Night Outside Boone's Adult Club*, 1993 (Spilling Black Ink, B-FEST Publications).

Lindsay Patterson's "A New Understanding" is from *Tarnished Hero*, 1986 (Modern Black Man).

Dedication

This book is dedicated to the elders: Grandparents, Luvenia "MaDear" Fears-Porchia and S. L. Porchia, who gave me to storytelling; and Adla Phillips-Mardis, who gave me to quilting. Praise to my mother, Rose Mitchell-Mardis Pinkney, who allowed me to steal her books in my youth, and my great-great uncle Moses Williams whose stories and cannon-like laughter will forever fill my heart. Lastly, I present this effort to my eldest sister, Deborah Mardis-Smith, as proof that she did not waste her time when reading Langston Hughes, et al., to me after school.

Each of these people, in their way, would say:

Remember the sound of what you love
One day you will hunger for such a simple thing.

Introduction

Of course I'd always known that I was black, but I'd never really stopped to take stock of what I was involved in. I met life as an individual and took my chances. . . . Through reading I was amazed to discover how confused people were.

Eldridge Cleaver, From "On Becoming," *Soul on Ice*

In many ways the above quote from Eldridge Cleaver, taken with liberties to context, makes a proper case for why this anthology, *KenteCloth: Southwest Voices of the African Diaspora*, is a necessary addition to the current re-facing of the African-American literary canon. Knowing that one is Black, African, African-American or any other layer of that Diaspora, requires understanding and appreciating that diversity. Cleaver, who hails from Wabbaseka, Arkansas, a region within the anthology's scope, used this quote to describe his awakening as a person of intentional action. I adopt his words here to cajole the reader's sensibilities to the untapped and oft purposefully overlooked literary culture of the Black Southwest region. Like Cleaver did with his essay, "On Becoming," I hope with this anthology to expand the reader's expectations, not merely of self, but rather of the developing canon.

This region—for our purposes defined as Texas and its contiguous states of Louisiana, Oklahoma, New Mexico and Arkansas—is truly untapped and underserved, as far as literature is concerned. Of course, this perspective concedes that the Southwest is at the mercy of others' appreciation of its contribution in this arena. None would deny that the Southwest has always been recognized for its wealth of contributions to the oral traditions. History is replete with the folklored endeavors of the trickster; preacher tales; superstitions; rhymes; riddles; spirituals and the like. The horrific ghost tales and vengeful slave yarns are rooted in this folklore and have been carried far and wide through black migration. Black comedy is the beneficiary of these Southern facets with its "hoo-ra" or "dozens." Black music, the ever-changing spiritual in particular, borrows its cadence from the stylized rhythms, speech and religious overtones of this region. However, somewhere along the path of usage these easily adopted cultural universals became the identifier of black backwardness.

In a lifetime lived throughout the Southwest region I have known these things, acts, ways of talking and of being, as a cherished, cultural essence. As youngsters we knew well the cultural and spiritual tales of black folks and heralded their rehashing in church and community endeavors. We drew heavily on the cultural sum and substance inherent in the pride-filled verbiage of black folklore and black speech. It was a time when cultural laughter dominated the relationships between black folks. Participating in something like "the dozens": a verbal contest of insults, or the street cornered, pre-rap verbal sparrings of "Shine," "Stagolee," or just plain singing, were preparation against the onslaught of the outside world. Much of this "inner-speak" utilized the negative identifier, "nigger," and in doing so it buffered the sting of the word from the mouths of others. Inherent in black culture-speak was a reliance on superstitions and popular general beliefs. Rhymes, as well, played an integral role in how the culture dealt with itself and the forces of upheaval and racial betterment that were reshaping it.

I have isolated these few cultural/literary genres because they are missing from the contemporary literature of most new black writers. Reading across the present-day offerings, I have been hard-pressed to recognize *remembrance* as a core element of this culture. From the first Griots, who kept the village stories for generations of Africans, to the *corner men* who "got it told" from day to day, incorporation of "the truth" has held a particular sway. However, the current literature from the Diaspora is reluctant to claim the once-universal thread of *what has been* in relationship to itself and the identity of its people/folk. Progression as a body of darker peoples is apparently costing much more than we once dared to imagine. A Langston Hughes poem heralded the way for many in the Diaspora who sought to put on the page what was once only spoken. It says, in part:

> Someday somebody's gonna stand up
> And talk about me

And write about me
Black and beautiful . . .
I reckon it'll be me myself
Yes, it'll be me.

However, in the ensuing years we have been sucked into the morass of a literary remaking of ourselves that parallels the European ideal. We are recreating ourselves on the page with the depth and breadth akin to a lost society. There are bits and pieces of memory that shade our images, but the rest is a caricature of the 'hood, ghetto, media-laden pimps, punks and perverts of which I, for one, have little recollection. Too many current correspondents of the Diaspora have merely regurgitated the scenes and sensibilities of a bedeviled America and placed them beneath a dark facade.

There is nothing greater in the legacy of black speak and pen that has served the culture better than remembrance. The legacy of remembering and retelling the tales of how we have come to the current state of being in the midst of oppression is what cores this Diaspora. Unfortunately, it is also what cleaves that core by creating the impression, among some, that the oral traditions and ways of the culture are backward and racially negative. The Southwest region is often an alluded reference. It states where we've been, but are also what we no longer connected to in any real sense. It is a claim of something that has been but is of little relevance to the present state of the African-American experience. It is "down home," "back there," "before the migration" and a passing reference to the relationships that *haunt* us as we try for a better life. It is no wonder that our young people have so eagerly accepted the face of doom and destruction. They have not seen reflected between the pages the faces of remembrance that tell them of themselves. They do not hear the tongue of remembrance in the stylized warbling of the songs. They are not called on to recite the chapter and verse of what was once a universal familiar. There was a time when the literature of the Diaspora provided answers for the only question that mattered: "Who are your people?"

It is here that Cleaver's notion invites the necessity of *KenteCloth: Southwest Voices of the African Diaspora*. The writers of this body are invested in intentional acts of inclusion and remembrance. They are invested in the realistic cycle of a culture. They are the breadth and width of being alive and flush with the ups and outs of moving the cultural body forward on the page. They are tested by the ugly embrace of snuff cans and a celebration of bare-chested black children running wild along the avenue. In short, they are challenged to griot. They are challenged to keep alive the stories of how we live instead of how we want the world to perceive our living. *KenteCloth* is the vehicle of "getting it told" on the page.

Herein are the children of a Black Southwest, like tornadoes are the siblings of wild night winds blowing at the urging of a full, mid-night moon. They come to you here, on the page, from storytellers, railroad bosses, liars, cooks, hairdressers, bus riders, singers, farm hands and the like. They tell the tales of fisher folk, ditch diggers, quilters and planters of trees. They come washed in the blood of the lamb and drenched in the wind-carried love of deep woods hollars and back alley brawls. They come immersed in a cacophony of prayers from childbirth to childhood and the laying down of the too young soul. They come strong from the womb of desolation disguised as charity and welcomed by the hands of fate. These are the writers of lives being lived and not of the merely imagined or coughed up writing class creations.

These mostly unpublished writers have fought and birthed and churched and gathered 'round gravesites, together. They have hunted the lakes, swamps, valleys and eyes of the racial beasts, together. They have come back again each year to honor their dead, together. They have wished for a passion and found it on the early morning dew of backyard pears, together. They have walked a mile and more in the brogan steppers of the elders, together. They have ratcheted out the long days and nights toward progression, where their voices have been abandoned for the smooth elegance of the other brother, together. They have endured silence together, and I am honored in accepting these wonderful and horrible and gloried voices of this brief collection. Each of these letters bears witness to the honor and discovery of being alive in a way that alive is not practiced today: Considered and Just.

Listen, as you read, for the lessons of those from whom we have come. Listen for the *"Shut up baby"* and *"Hush now"* that both soothed and taught the lessons of patience and honor in childhood. Hear these voices traveling across the generations and migrations and histories and oceans. Nothing of the remembrance is lost among these writers. The elders may be gone in body, but their lessons linger in the living and sharing of these stories, poems and plays. Listen for the voices come to the page; the oral dance of tongue to teeth and song to heart. The oral tradition is not Rap's raucous sound, nor is it the latest hip-hop machinations of makeshift Gospel/spirituals that permeate the minds of the young. The oral tradition is born of remembrance.

As a child I, like these contributors, sat at the feet of my elders in my grandparents' parlor and drank in the stories. Afterwards, my grand-mother would lean down and say,

> *Remember these stories. Someday the noise of your life will try to drown them out, but remember the stories of how we made it through. Today you are twelve and a lover of stories, but one day you will not be twelve. Remember the sound of what you love. One day you will hunger for such a simple thing!*

In preparing this manuscript I heard clearly the noise that Grand-mother MaDear spoke of those many years ago. She is gone now, but the lessons of that parlor remain. She, like all the others who touched the lives of these writers, said, "Remember," as if they knew the day of forgetting would be upon us. "Remember," as if someday the culture, the Diaspora, would have to make remembering an intentional act.

Welcome to *KenteCloth*, an intentional act.

Jas. Mardis, Editor

WITNESSES

Witnessing is a religious act shared by all peoples of the Diaspora, but especially across the Bible Belt that includes *KenteCloth*'s Southwest scope. Witnessing is also an act of life whereby we share the legacies, fears, hopes and stories of the people from whom we have come.

This selection of writers is the best of what the Southwest has to offer the world in the "call to witness." Though they do not always employ a direct religious overtone in their writing, these authors may invoke the spirit in other ways. Their literary voices are as unique and varied as the hues of their skin. Their choice of subjects offers an equally varied glimpse into the region's vast cache of truly new voices.

BERNESTINE SINGLEY

Bearing Witness

I look at Desiree.

"The last place I want to be is around a sick momma," I say.

"I know what you mean," Desiree replies, looking sympathetic.

"Oh, well," I continue, "the universe puts us in places where we need to be. But . . ." I sigh heavily. Suddenly, we change the subject. Talk of food and what lies ahead sends sorrow scurrying.

We have gathered, six women friends and I, to catch up after seven years apart. As night turns day and day turns night again, bared souls skitter across the hot skillet of confession. Jubilant, weeping, anxious, hopeful, fearful, fragile warrior sisters of steel.

Stories tumble over each other until, without warning, they crash into the clock and it is time to leave.

Desiree and I climb into Pat's Land Rover for the ride across town.

I rest my head against the window and force myself not to think about Pat's mom waiting at the other end, fresh from major surgery, hooked to an oxygen tank, a metal tree with tubes for stems and leaves of plastic bags, the smells, the sounds, the sights blaring the message of human frailty.

Mommas can die. Odessa, my momma, is dead. This is not a truth of which I want to be reminded even two years after the fact.

I twist in the front passenger's seat and listen to Desiree and Pat. I wrap myself in the rhythm of their sounds, comforting, loving, caring, strong, brilliant, deep, skimming surfaces, plumbing depths, guffaws, sighs.

I love these women. My friends. One from Brooklyn by way of Baltimore, the other a South Central Los Angeles transplant to Chicago's Hyde Park. I love being in the darkness of the jeep with the lights all around, the dirty snow flying by outside the window.

The Chicago skyline unfolds in front of us like a surround-sound Omnimax theater experience. I miss Chicago. A real city.

I love the expressway and the cars filthy from the salt and grime of big city winter. I am happy with the grayness, the exhaust fumes, the bone-chillingness of it all.

Content, cozy, I begin to doze. On cue, sorrow slips into that space between sleep and dreaming and snatches me back to consciousness.

Sick momma. Oh, God, I don't want to see a sick momma. I don't want to smell a sick momma. I don't want to hear a sick momma. I want Pat's momma to get up and not be sick.

I hope that Pat's momma will not drop me to the floor again.

I have seen a sick momma before. My momma was sick. And then she died. It didn't scare me. I was stunned. For months I walked around in a daze of denial until one day I couldn't stand up quite as straight as usual. The next day, I was bent over further still. By the fourth day, I was crawling around on my hands and knees. I couldn't stand up at all.

The doctors pulled and stretched. Moist heat, electrodes, mechanical contraptions lifted my body first this way then that, day after day.

Finally, at home one day, I unfolded myself gingerly onto the floor. I rolled to one side. That was a mistake. A torrent of water gushed from my eyes. Rivers of snot bubbled from my nose. I was suffocating in water. What to do?

In a few days, I stood straight enough to board a plane. Warmed by the Jamaican sun, soothed by the ocean, basking in the generous love of the blessing who is my husband, gradually I stood taller and taller until one day, I was no longer bent and twisted by grief.

For two years, I have kept a wide stride. But now I am scared.

Pat whips the jeep into the exit lane and I begin to pray. *Dear God, please don't let Pat's momma drop me to the floor again.*

We pull into Pat's driveway. Once inside, we are immediately enveloped in the unbridled excitement and instant love of children for company. Jacqueline, five going on twenty-five, and I fall immediately in love with each other. Victoria, seven, and Desiree stake their mutual claims. Jay, nine and full of male wisdom, stays out of sight, wary of being swept into this circle of very noisy women.

The girls lead us to the third floor. Passing the second floor landing, I keep my head averted because I know that Pat's sick momma is there somewhere. No one has told me this, but I can feel it on my skin.

The next morning, on my way downstairs, I pause barefoot on the second floor landing. It is very, very quiet. There's a door ajar ahead of me, off to the left. I know this is where Pat's momma is. I head for the door, but stop at the entry.

I listen, barely able to hear above the pounding of my heart. I see a leg partially covered by a beautiful fluffy comforter with tiny blue flowers sprinkled all over it. Sunlight fills the room. I don't move. I close my eyes and listen.

I am not breathing.

When I hear the housekeeper's footsteps, I tip backwards from the doorway and on downstairs to the first floor landing. I barely have the strength to lace my boots and make it out the front door.

Several hours later, I return. Jacqueline greets me at the front door all smiles and five-year-old jumping. I practice the words under my breath until I'm finally able to ask Jacqueline very casually, "So, how's Grandma?"

She looks at me wisely and with concern says, "Not too good."

As we climb the stairs to the second landing, I ask her, "Do you think we should check on Grandma?" She nods yes and promptly skips into the room with the flowered comforter. I follow her, but stop at the entry.

I hear a moaning rattle. I stop breathing. I've heard this sound before.

I cross the threshold and see Jacqueline at the head of the bed fluttering kisses across her Grandma's forehead.

I move close to the bed and, without thinking, begin to rub the leg still partially uncovered. I practice the words inside my head.

Finally, I say, "Mrs. Boatright, can I get you anything?" I'm not sure she can hear me.

I am startled by the voice so clear and strong that comes back at me. "That's okay, baby. Thank you for asking. I'm fine."

Her voice drowns out the moaning rattle. But as soon as she stops, it starts again. I want her to keep talking.

Instead I say, "C'mon, Jacqueline, let's let Grandma get some rest."

Jacqueline promises her Grandma that she will check on her later. Then, she grabs my hand and pulls me down the stairs.

Hours later, we set out for the airport with Jacqueline in the back seat, wedged between an exercise mat and my carry-on bag.

While Pat and I do our best to talk over her head, Jacqueline leans forward to play with her mom's earring. She caresses first Pat's face, then mine. Without warning, she leans even farther forward and kisses us both. Then she sits back, smug with the love she has bestowed.

"Momma believes she's going to die," Pat whispers from the side of her mouth.

"Mommas know when they're going to die," I whisper back. "And you know what? You can't keep them here once they've decided to go."

Pat's eyes widen, glistening. She tells me of a premonition she'd had a month earlier, a sign, she thought, of her momma's impending death.

I remember my own remarkably similar experience. The tearful torrent that swept in from nowhere one cloudless, sky blue day and forced me off the road. A month later, Odessa was dead.

I think back to the moaning rattle earlier this day on Pat's second floor landing. But I keep this to myself and hope it doesn't mean what I know it means.

At home the next day, I am exhausted and sleep all day long. Sick mommas, dead mommas, can wear you out.

Finally, I drag myself awake. I call Pat to ask about her momma.

"Momma is dead, Bernestine. She died this afternoon at 3:30." This is said with such matter-of-factness that I am stunned.

But relief follows swiftly when Pat's next utterance is lost in sobbing.

The universe puts us in the places where we need to be.

TIM SEIBLES

Bridge of Silk

Tim, this is Talib. You knew me
as Teddy Winborne. When you
get a chance, call me.

This message and variations left 3 times
in about 36 hours. Three calls.
Long distance. While I was out of town.

We had grown up together, me and Teddy,
listening to Hendrix, playing basketball.

Not best friends but good friends: teenaged boys
here and there pretending to be Bruce Lee.

It had been twenty-some years since we
took the subway downtown to see "Fist of Fury."

Teddy was now Talib Abdeen Bahar,
A Muslim who ran a small insurance office.

When we were kids he could say things to his mom
that would have cost me my life.

We never phoned long distance ever.

We would ride the XH bus to school.
The Germantown High girls would be packed on there
with their foxy, fish-netted selves.

We were pretty cool. I mean, we
weren't afraid of girls. We'd say,

Hey, baby, you know it would be a
really dynamite thing   if you and me   could maybe
lay, play and   parlay sometime.

I'm not sure what we were doing,
but we were young brothers in Philly
back in the day of *The Dells* and *The Chi-Lites*:

La-la la-la la-la la-la-la means . . .
we had to have some lines.
Like a bridge of silk   between us and the girls.

It had been a long, long time.
Late 60s, early 70s.

Black barbers gave us "blow outs"
to make our afros bigger.

Gangs—Downtown, Haines Street, Brickyard, The Clang—
When somebody said, "Where you from,"
it meant which corner.

Our parents probably should've kept us in the house
for the rest of our lives.

I'm 40 and starting to go bald.
I get home—three messages from Teddy.

He used to keep a slight scowl on his face,
but you really had to if you didn't want to get
"messed with."

I mean, you go down around the way
beaming like *Wally* and *Beaver Cleaver*—
you'd get your ass kicked every day.

And we didn't want that. We wanted to be hard.
We wore high-top *Cons* and sharkskin slacks.
We said, *"Fuck you"* and *"Hey, man, fuck all that."*

When we body-boxed you could feel the fist-prints for days.

I don't see why we ever grew up at all.
That distance between 12 and 21—a couple blocks,
just a curtain of beads.

And what did it get us?   Older.

Deeper into the world's gaping snarl.
Sometimes Teddy would bring his bass out on the porch
and play till Mrs. Thomas came out and crossed her arms.

Some days we'd be in the schoolyard playing two-on-two
till those bent rims damn near disappeared in the dark.

Three calls in two days   after a million years.

From Talib Abdeen Bahar   a.k.a.   Theodore Winborne.

So, I'm an inch from
dialing but the phone
rings. My mother clears
her throat, says
some guy shot Teddy
yesterday—some guy
walked into the office and
killed Teddy. Wednesday.

Afternoon. Somebody that he
knew. Walked in. Shot
him. In the head. Right
there. Blood everywhere.

Once I saw him and Gary Cooke do this deep blues in Melvin's
basement.

We were all around 15. Just before the block party. Summer.
It was hot down there—like the inside of somebody's sweatpants—
but they jammed,   so we stayed.

I wonder what Mr. Bahar wanted to tell me.

He was bow-legged; he'd wear baggy khakies to hide that
sometimes.

I mean, if somebody like Teddy
leaves you a message

seems like you should get a chance
to call him back.

VICKY CHARLESTON

the promise

we stand before the mirror,
he, falling into puberty;
me, teaching the joys
of oily skin and the history
of pimples.101
when suddenly
I notice the height.
he, now taller than me
by a full inch and I wonder
how could it be,
when only two weeks before
we stood in front of
this very same mirror
in this very same place
in this very same way
and it was not so,
how quickly they grow
and go on . . .
and he,
sensing my anxiety
calmly says,
"don't worry mom,
i'll write. I promise."

MAWIYAH KAI EL-JAMAN BOMANI

taboo

she slapped my hand
as I pointed to the tube
of ruby red
the same ruby red
that the light skin girl
had just paid
a whole dollar twenty-five for
the same ruby red
that had fourteen-year-old girls
willing to boycott
the local k and b drug store
if forced to suffer through another day with naked lips
when news spread
a new shipment was in
better get yours
a-s-a-p
I was second in line
I wanted my first tube to last forever
so I came prepared
laid my three dollars down on her counter
and said
ma'm i'll take two tubes of your ruby red

listen girl
she said
didn't your mama teach you anything
you can't go around with your lips painted red
don't you look in the mirror every morning
can't you see
you too black

for what I got
and besides
red is the devil's color
red is for whores
with the possible exception
of high yellas
who can slide
cause society recognizes
how our color
compliments any color
but you
she laughed
don't nobody got what you need
except maybe
the baby aisle
I recommend you buy yourself some vaseline
for those chapped lips
go home forget about ruby red
and please
dry those eyes
you have nobody to blame
but your mama
matter of fact
you should be thanking me
it was up to your mama to hip you
to the taboo
cause everybody round here knows
that black black girls
ain't suppose to wear red

A New Understanding

"Gawddamit," I says to Teddy, "we gonna git up the Vigilantes and go over and beat the hell outa that Hitler."

"How we gonna git over there?" Teddy says to me.

"We git over alright. Don't worry 'bout that," I says.

"I dunno," says Teddy. "That's maybe further'n New Orleans, and 'sides, you gotta cross lotsa water."

"Hell," I says, "when somebody wants to do something aint no water gonna stop 'em."

"I dunno," says Teddy.

"You just don't tell nobody," I says. "You jest don't tell nobody, 'cause if they find out what we're planning to do, they jest might send some spy to wipe us all out."

"Maybe we ought'n do nothing, Bo," Teddy says.

"You jest don't tell nobody. Let me figure out ever'thing."

"What if some spy hear us talking now?" says Teddy.

Me and Teddy quickly git up from the hay in top of our barn and we look through the cracks, but we don't see nothing but Ma hanging out the wash. We both sit back down and I decide to roll me a cigarette outa corn silk; only after I done it I find I don't have any matches and Teddy don't have none either. But we sit and pretend that we smoke anyway. I take a few puffs and I hand it to Teddy.

"You know, Teddy," I says, "if we git up the Vigilantes and go and beat that Hitler, maybe we never hafta go to school again."

"I dunno, Bo," says Teddy, "it look like we gotta go to school all the time, 'til we grown."

"Shoot," I says to Teddy, "you jest mark my words. I aint never going to school again."

"Your papa gonna have something to say 'bout that," says Teddy, like my papa was the meanest man in the world.

"If I don't wanna go, he can't make me."

"Your papa aint gonna stand for that, he being a school teacher."

"You jest wait til September."

"Okay," says Teddy, "but knowing your papa he don't take nothing from nobody."

Just then Ma calls me. She never calls me Bo like other people do. She always got to holler out my full name, Bartholomew!

"Yes'm, I'm coming," I tell her. I tell Teddy I see him later, and if he breathes a word about the Vigilantes to anybody I take revenge.

Ma is sitting on the back porch in her rocker and, as I near the porch a chicken get in my way and I kick at it.

"Don't you do that, Bartholomew!" Ma yells. "Those chickens have feelings just like you!"

"Yes'm," I says.

"How many times have I told you to say 'yes ma'am' and not 'yes'm.'"

"Yes'm. I mean, yes ma'am."

"Your father's going to town," Ma says. "You want to go with him?"

"God yes," I say.

"Don't blaspheme, Bartholomew, or you won't go," Ma says.

"No ma'am," I say, "but he gonna buy me?"

"You'll see when you get there," Ma says.

Papa come out and he got on his best suit like he going to church. I ask him where we go since he so dressed up, and he say we go first to the Board of Education where he got to sign a contract.

Me and Pa walk up the highway, and if we had walked down the highway we'd have run right smack into New Orleans.

"Papa," I says, as I grab his hand, "what about that Hitler? What if he come over here?"

"It'll be a sad day, son," Papa says. He walked so fast that I could hardly keep up.

"Don't you think we oughta go over there and git him first?"

"We're trying, son," says Papa.

"You think we gonna be able to git him without any help?" I ask him.

Papa didn't answer me right away. He look down at me and grin like he always does when he knows I got something in my head. He said: "What you got in that mind of yours this time, Bo?"

"Nothing, Pa," I says. "I jest don't like that Hitler man."

"He's a wicked, wicked man, but our armies'll take care of him. One man can't do the job alone." Papa look down at me and wink his eye and then he pat me on the head. "My crazy Bo," he says laughing. Jest then we come to Miz Carrie's house and she is sitting on her porch fanning herself.

"Howdy, Miz Carrie," Papa says, tipping his hat, but Miz Carrie hardly speaks to him. I guess she was still mad at what I done to her last Sunday. I'd always heard that she wore a wig, 'cause she was as bald as an eagle, and since I was sitting behind her last Sunday I couldn't resist seeing if it was true. She bawled like a baby and I couldn't help but cry too.

"Bo," Papa says, "speak to Miz Carrie."

"Hullo," I say real soft, 'cause I'm really honestly sorry 'bout pulling off her wig in front of the whole church.

We get to the Board of Education, which is in a big stone building with twenty-nine steps to climb. Papa go into the office and leave me outside, telling me to behave myself and act like a gentleman til he gits back.

While I'm standing there minding my own business, this little red-haired white kid come out of the office and up to me. He has lumps all over his face and wire on his teeth. He ask me my name.

"Bo," I tell him.

"What's your Christian name?" He ask me.

"Turner," I tell him.

"You a nigger," he say to me.

"No I a man!" I tell him.

"You talk like a nigger and look like a nigger," he says to me, "so that makes you a nigger."

"What's a nigger?" I ask him.

"I just told you, stupid," he say to me.

"You ain't told me nothing," I says.

"Niggers are stupid," he says. "My papa says so."

"Your papa don't know what he talking 'bout," I says.

"My papa the smartest man in the world. He's the Superintendent of Education."

"That don't make him the smartest man in the world."

"It does, too," he say.

"It don't," I say.

"It does, too!"

"It don't!"

He hit me on the arm and I hit him back. He continue to hit me and I let him, 'cause I knew I could lick him with one good punch he was so skinny. But I got tired of him hitting me so I let him have it in the stomach and he bent over and held his stomach and start to wail. When he got his breath, he ran back into the Board of Education and came back with his papa and mine.

"What happened, Bo!" my Papa yells.

"He hit me," I say to him.

"I didn't hit him," the skinny kid moans, like he's about to die. "He just hit me for no reason at all."

"You a lie," I say.

"Don't you say that!" my papa yells at me.

"He is a lie," I say, "'cause I was minding my own business when he come up and hit me."

"Papa," the skinny say, "he hit me for no reason at all."

"You'd better do something with that boy of yours, James," the skinny kid's papa says to mine.

The skinny kid come up to me and my papa hold my hands behind my back. He hit me in the face a couple of times as hard as he can, and then he kick me on the leg. I try to get away from my papa so I can defend myself, but my papa hold me so tight that I can't do nothing. After the skinny kid finish hitting me he thumb his nose and scoots into the Board of Education.

"I'm so sorry Mister Foster," my papa says to the Superintendent of Education, "and when I get him home I'm gonna give him the beating of his life."

"I think he's learned his lesson now," says the Superintendent, who was red-haired and had lumps all over his face, too.

My papa bows his head at the Superintendent, then catches me by the arm and nearly drags me down the twenty-nine steps. When we get off the Board of Education grounds, he let me go.

"Let's go to Woolworth's and buy some peppermint," my papa say in a voice so low I can hardly hear him.

"I'm not hungry," I snap.

He don't say nothing, but we go into Woolworth's and buy the biggest bag of peppermint I'd ever seen. We get back on the highway and start for home, but all I can think about is how long it will take to walk to New Orleans and how I can get a boat to take me and the Vigilantes over to where that Hitler feller is, then kill him and ever'body in his army and never come back. But I look up at my pa and his eyes are red like he'd been crying. I shift my bag of peppermint to my left hand and I take his hand. He smiles down at me and I smile back.

"Papa," I ask, "is that Hitler man white?"

CHARLEY MOON

THE BLUEBIRD LOUNGE

. . . PERCY SLEDGE IS ON THE JUKEBOX, AND THE LIGHTS ARE SO LOW THAT THE NEON MILLER BEER SIGN SEEMS TO LIGHT UP THE WHOLE BAR AS THE LOCALS STROLL IN . . . EACH ONE SPORTING THEIR LATEST OUTFIT; THE WOMEN WITH THEIR CHEWING GUM A-POPPIN AND SHINY EARBOBS GLISTENING IN THE DIM LIGHT . . . SOMEONE LIGHTS A CIGARETTE . . . THIS PLACE SMELLS LIKE STALE BEER, CHEAP COLOGNE AND DIRTY ASHTRAYS . . . THE WOMAN BEHIND THE BAR IS THE OWNER . . . SHE'S OVERWEIGHT AND LOOKS LIKE SHE'S SEEN SOME THINGS AND ALWAYS KEEPS HER REVOLVER AT ARM'S REACH UNDERNEATH THE BAR. . . .
. . . THE KITCHEN DOOR SWINGS OPEN AND A MAN STEPS THROUGH CARRYING A BUS TUB TO COLLECT THE DIRTY DISHES . . . HE'S THE DISHWASHER; AN OLD GENTLEMAN WHO LOOKS LIKE HE'S BEEN ON A TWO-WEEK DRUNK, AND JUST MIGHT STILL BE IN THE MIDDLE OF IT, WITH TWO DAYS GROWTH OF BEARD. . .
. . . THEN A MAN WALKS THROUGH THE FRONT DOOR AND OVER TO A COUPLE SITTING AND TALKING AT ONE OF THE TABLES . . . HE LEANS OVER TO THE WOMAN AND SPEAKS SOFTLY INTO HER EAR . . . AS HE SPEAKS HE GENTLY PATS HER ON THE BACK . . . PATTING HER BACK . . . PATTING HER BACK . . . PATTING HER BACK . . . PAT . . . PAT . . . PAT. . . . THEN HE TURNS AND STROLLS OUT OF THE LOUNGE THE SAME WAY HE WALKED IN, WITHOUT A LOOK BACK. . . . AND AS THE DOOR SWINGS SHUT BEHIND HIM . . . THE WOMAN WITH WHOM HE HAD BEEN TALKING AND PATTING . . . PATTING . . . PATTING AND TALKING COLLAPSES FACE DOWN ON THE TABLE . . . DEAD . . . IN FRONT OF HER FRIEND . . . DEAD . . . BEFORE THE AMBULANCE CAN BE CALLED . . . BEFORE ANYONE IN THE BAR EVEN NOTICES . . . DEAD . . . FROM MULTIPLE STAB WOUNDS TO THE BACK. . . .

VALERIE BRIDGEMAN-DAVIS

Scatting to Heaven's Gate
For Ella Fitzgerald

When Ella died at 78,
her notes floated out
swinging and scatting
in perfect pitch,

extemporaneously,
like her living,
without effort
and improvising
the lines

scatting up and down
the scales, her voice
the perfect instrument,
her life as jazzy
as her songs:

Lady Be Good and
shoobee-doobee-doo-ow!
A Tisket, A Tasket
and in her own life
a basket full of problems

She could cut the air
sharp like a talon
with her tongue,
put music to Cole Porter
and the Duke,

composing on
the moment

singing encores into the heat
of the night
that Black Bird of Song
Ella.

At The Victory Grill, No. 1

For the poets

Gathering in a circle
around tables, empty
except for our charged
dreams

the call comes, a wave
across oceans, rivers
or words come calling:

sing to us, sing to us
our lives
tell our stories,
prophets, griots
hear the voices emerge
from our own skin

while we gather, light reflect
in anticipation of the tattered fabric
of our quilted lives, woven
together are the hard questions
with the soft bodies

covered in torrential tears
and lazy summer cool-aid days
the heat, hot and hotter
of our variegated black passion

we giggle or softly smile,
frown or loudly amen
as each story taps into
our own ancient warehouse

of memories
I've been there, we've been here,
we've all been here before

or, I have never heard Miles
except on long drives
back to Alabama
with miles ahead,
but I'm glad you saw his back
on stage that time

we sit, hugging each other's words
as they float into the air
changing space from church
to chamber, street dancin' in N'Oleans
to that deep place inside us all,
the darkest of the deep passions
surface

and we never allow each other to forget
that the personal is political,
correctly speaking

to die, to live, is to make choices—
can you stand them?

It is not simply our late-coming voices
in the air, but "God stepped out
on space" and James is
in the circle, too

we bring our lovers with us
even when there is no rhyme to it
and honor all the Old People,
the Elders, Papas, Mamas

Who loved us, love us still
even though we've lost the skill
to make medicine from the earth
or cook the best batch
of Sunday cornbread and beans

EMILY M. NEWSOME

Close Don't Count

I was riding along, reading about your kind, a bag hugged between
my feet and another held secure by a well-placed elbow. I was
assured of not moving from my seat by the two ample-hipped sisters
on either side. One was still rolling her eyes because I sat down next
to her, the other munching on fries, having turned her back as best
she could, so as not to be rude, I imagine. (She didn't offer the rest of
us any.)
I saw you get on.
Another bright-skinned, eyes full of vision, curly-headed wonder.
I went back to my book.
The bus rolled on. Folks got on and got off. The eye roller charged
forward trying to make her connection, and I moved down, nodding
to the deacon from my church, and then ignoring him.
I wanted to finish reading about your kind.
Another sister got on, and you stood up to give her your seat. She
took another, and you sat back down. I looked at you, and smiled,
and nodded my head. "Well done," the nod said, "and thank you, on
behalf of all the sisters everywhere who worked real hard today, and
would really appreciate a seat on an overcrowded, running late bus."
And you smiled back. And I went back to my book.
I felt your eyes on me, and I looked up and smiled weakly again,
only to see you looking eager. I nodded, more curtly this time,
hoping you would understand that you had already received your
reward.
I went back to my book.
And you peered again.
And I peeped again.
And we both smiled again.
And I went back to my book.
(You don't get it, do you?)

The bus rolled on, and my stop came (thank you!) and as I rose to get off, deacon in tow, you craned your head above the others and mouthed "Can I go to?"

I smiled at you and turned my head, disappointed.

You were close.

But close don't count.

GLENN JOSHUA

chapter one: a social black music art lesson

we used to sing with fire
trumpets and drummers, pianissimos and playwrights
smoked up blue note thunderstorms.

we used to force open the closed venetian blinds of black minds
whenever we poeted and danced.
and the people would be checking us out,
inhaling our vibes and inventions, calling us everything,
including the sacred children of god.

within our artistry, you could very well find a horn or a pen
in each well rehearsed hand.
bass clarinet reeds crooned in sweet middle passage registers,
spiritually introducing personal letters dedicating our lives with
songs, these tunes, composed in unstandard seventh string choral structures
were named, "God's Dark Babies Makin' Love in Two A.M. Rain."

our down home harmonies were tempered by mississippi
delta dirt roads and sunday afternoon jubilee revivals.
our grooves used to groove past the brass of chicago's blue collar
working class, shoutin' hallelujah, hippin universes with a
complexity simplified, forever revering the corona of illuminated
psychological stratospheres.

i'm talking about the sixties in black arts inspiring alternate ages.
boogie downs and second lines on every city block jumpin' funky.
nine point flowers expanding tempo from off beat duct tape connected
bass horns and cow bells, bombarding basin bourbon and beale streets
with black rhythms, and its happening again right now.
revisionary blackness. or better yet, the explosion of kinetic energy replaying

revitalized reverb for you.
can you hear it? hear us celebrating ourselves with unique harmonic rituals?
jazz hip rhythm and blues gospel and classical works are reconstructed
every time one of us opens our big black minds.
our golden transitions are doo wops cut on hot wax and cool parchment.
earth tales are sung and written in our very own language because ancient
black art is still young.
our stories are delicate diaries dancing in melodic cotton fields where
    blossoms are harvested to clothe our heritage,
just like the warm, comforting embrace or new
found awareness.
we create whether it's humorous, serious, tragic, truthful,
mythic, exhilarating, or thoughtful.

we're bathed in sonia sanchez's tears,
immersed in pharaoh sander's saxophone winds,
baptized in amiri baraka's breath and
we still sing with fire.

our fragrant breezes are the sixties shifting seeds
predicting our own unified future, reminding brothers
and sisters that singing is the underground sound,
and creativity is our roots to chapter two
which is up to you

IFE NZINGHA TALIBAH MAHDI

ONE FRIDAY NITE AT BOONE'S ADULT CLUB

was long haired jheri-curled musicians
tired lookin' bra-less bar maids
a slow sensuous saxophone played
by a bro. with hair longer than mine

high priced watered down drinks
gigglin' ladies &
married men tryin' to "cop"
big, burly, pistol-totin' bouncers
a female singer who, God knows
wasn't no Aretha

red-eyed spaced out brothers
selling "wolf" tickets
sistuhs wearin'
red satin & mink

& 4 white chicks sittin' with some
brothers in a
boothinthebackinthecornerinthedark

& the brothers looked like they had
died & gone straight to Heaven . . .

straight to heaven

Slow Dancing

Thru the bluelight haze of
the crowded basement
I watch you
& the cocoa butter
brown/ness of you

                  tantalizes my taste buds

You ask me to dance
& we cross the room
yr touch is a live wire
as you take me in yr arms

chest to breast/breast to chest
& knee-deep in funk
we begin the dance

I can feel yr heartbeat

              through the sheerness
              of my blouse

so much like my own
native drums
it gets me caught up
and it's all I can do
to stay on my feet

you got me
swaying, yr male scent
has me dizzy & I'm
full of mischief
& expectation
longing for the thrill
of yr touch (on a deeper level,
if you know what I mean, & I think
you do)

I feel yr hot breath
on my neck
its warmth
drawing me deeper
into the safety of yr chest
again I feel
weak
my knees/
begin to buckle

chest to breast/
breast to chest
knee deep in funk
         slow dancing

with nothin' on our minds

but each other

               & how to end this dance
               w/our clothes still on

VON

Just Burn Me

If I don't show up at your funeral, don't take it personally. It's just that I don't want to remember you that way. Neither do I want you to ever envision me lying in some decorated box in a nice church dress with my hands resting on my stomach. That's not me at all.

It seems that every time I think about someone who has died, the first picture my memory can recollect is the one where they are lying on their backs with some imitation smile on their faces similar to those found in high school yearbooks.

Just burn me. Nobody knows me better than myself. I fix my own hair. Pick out my own clothes. Do my own make-up. So I figure if I do it just the way I like it while I'm living, I don't want nobody else doing it when I'm dead. Hell, I can't even get a hair stylist to fix my hair the right way now, so I damn sure ain't going to allow them to experiment on me when they know I can't complain about it afterwards.

And it's not about me caring what you think of my appearance when I'm dead. I couldn't care less what you think. I just know that my soul will not rest after experiencing the complications of a church funeral. I don't wear dresses, unless they fall high above my knees. God forbid they put me in panties *or* pantyhose. The only pennies I keep on me are in the ashtray of my car, so I don't want any up under my eyes. And if I'm lying on my back, nine times out of ten there's a black man somewhere in close proximity between my nose and my toes . . . and if I'm by myself, you best believe my hands are not resting on my stomach. So unless yall can funeralize me standing up with my hands on my hips, eyes wide open accompanied by a sassy smile with my big afrocentric earrings giving life to my ears, and my African shells tightly adorning my ankles . . . just burn me. I stand for far too many things to be represented on my back. I'm always on my feet, and I don't take shit lying down.

Don't enslave the spirit of my soul beneath the surface of this foreign soil, engraved with the footprints of the overseer and the hooves of the mule that never, ever galloped across his forty acres and the wheels of the wagon that carried the master to the auction of the slave block where he branded the spirit which reincarnated me. No. Don't bury me here. For I've had a lifelong funeral complete with a constant burial surrounded by hundreds of wilted flowers. So at my death, re-member my life. Remember how I smiled with open eyes during the wake of the funeral of my life. Remember the way I dodged each shovel of dirt the gravedigger forcefully threw at me, how I always came up through the mud. No, don't bury me here. Grant me the eternal peace that can only be found in the freedom of the wind. And I'll see you when you get there.

nia akimbo

getting a word in, edge-wise
(for Constance)

I think he's homeless

she says to me
as we sat
waiting
for the light to

change while he
clad in wafer thin pants
and shirt sockless shoes
sans lace

arms draped about
a skeletal frame
shielding little against
a brisk winter wind

waited
for any change.

Look how bright the lights are
The season is upon us before
long Santa will come, now
here's the place we meet
our friends

softly assuredly
she speaks again:

I think

she begins and I interrupt

Come, join the fun

but she refused
a favorite drink sat
alone she said

to think till finally
this scene is done
and night's trek
home a reward

until i see him
or someone like him—
thankful she is asleep
and will not witness
as i ignore the spectacle
who has ruined our evening

with his reminder
of loss and losing
even when all has gone.

home now and safely
nestled in bed she wakens
her concern honed by comfort
her eyes burning into mine

I'm sure he's homeless
What will we do about it?

META CARSTARPHEN

Corner Courtship

do wah
do wah do harmonies embrace
hot summer sidewalks:
night brings street corner lights
in place of moon rays to shine
upon Love's couriers:

> do wah
> do wah do wah
> so fi-ine yeah

brick two-stories make
acoustical magic/shooting
five voices/high/into the sky
to reverberate back in one
blended siren call:

> I say
> my baby's so doggone fine
> send those chills up'ndown
> my spine:
> do wah do wah yeah
> so fine

little foxes dance on stage
pirouetting in denim delights/
abbrieviated tops 'n
carefully pressed 'dos/
trying to be so fine/just

fine enuff to trap a
special tune their way:

                           sing it baby uuhh
                           sing it uuhh uuhh
                           hit it like that
                           do it like this
                           sing it sing it sing it baby
                           sing it fo' me

appreciative admirers
egg the chorus on, and the
do wahs git louder/
escalating to a shrill finess
sharp enough to slice
the coolest heart/trap
the youngest vamp into
experienced submission 'n
convince the faithless of
romance's potent miracle:

                           do wah
                           do wah for you

young to-be lovers
steal a special verse
for ownership/
imagining all the profundities
of lovemaking that
by day
teen lips shyly avoid:

                           do wah means I love you

for a few evening moments
city girls become
gentry country/serenaded
by the pauper princes
of the block:

                                        do wah so
                                        why do I do

till
curfew stops the show/clears the
curbside theater of
giddy listeners who
sashay back home to a
mundane reality:

& in the bedded night
do wahs
are echoes now/circling
themselves dimly in
the cycle of sleep/sounding
like this:

do wah good night
my love   do wah
sleep tight   do wah
my love   doo wah . . .

ANA SISNET

Son of a Distant God

In the beginning was the question . . .
followed by another.
In the beginning
no one had answers.

He was, he said,
alone.

He believes, he says,
he left
a part of himself dead
with his friend that night.

Riding and riding through
swift, unsuspecting puddles
until there was light
until there was light
until he heard voices
until he felt, he said,
no longer alone.

Foot soldier,
son of a god
son of a god in the making.
Unrecognized holiness
in the skin of the black god-boy
on the bus.

If you listen
he will tell you, he says,

he remembers his name,
his name bigger than his birthweight,
his name commanding him to rise.
He will tell you, he says,
he remembers the time
before he was reborn
the son of a distant god.

Until then, he yearns
for a family
for an easy life
for pyramids among the projects.
He is a foot soldier in a god's army,
searching for the best light
searching for the keys
searching for the way
to the million niggahs he carries in himself
the million niggahs not yet free
from jails, from prisons,
from behind him.

Black and male and American today
he will perhaps forgive
but never accept that he is the son
of a failed scientist
and a mother full of words. Human parents
offering no logic
no answers
to their son of a distant
god.

TIM SEIBLES

Wha'chu Shoulda Told the Brother

Yo, nigga, it don't have ta be like that—I mean,
a brotha miss a stop sign, he jus miss the mothafucka,
tha's all. It ain't like I hit that raggedy-ass,
neva-seen-a-car-wash, can-I-get-a-sunroof, three-tires-
an-a-Bigwheel ride you got.
                              If I had I'd halfway understan
all that I'll-kick-yo-nappy-ass attitude you run up on me wit.
But see, you can't give a brotha a break, so fuck you
and the two punk-ass toads you hopped in on! Runnin aroun
lookin like Dennis Rodman-meets-Godzilla—like ta scared me
And my car: face all scrunched up ginst my window, nasty
rat teef all snaggled up and yella—

                              Tartar Control Crest
done definitely loss control a' yo ass and Right Guard too,
stanky muhfucka.

                              Gotdam, baby, can't you see it's jus me—
another black man tryin ta keep his eyes on the prize, tryin
ta keep from bein COLORED right out the picture. I mean
I'm here in America with more than traffic on my mind,
know what I'm sayin? Either my head's gonna get bigger
or it's gonna blow up, yo. You see how it is.

                              I mean,
sometimes, man, all we got is each other—like right now—
here we are at this intersection with nothing

but ourselves and two cars
ready to take us either way.
                        Maybe we were supposed to meet
here, 43rd and Granby, this corner, like a brief mecca
where stupidity skids to a sudden stop, where two men might wake up
and recognize each other as reluctant kin.
                             Maybe this was a
benign hiccup of the universe, brother—the Dharma in action.
I mean, if we hadn't nearly collided we would be
miles away by now, still complete strangers,
                                 and I've been
feeling a little too strange for a little too long already,
know what I mean? I mean
I think you understand the situation—
how everything American piles on,
how the nation has a choke-hold
on some of us,
                    how every sunrise is another
hard shove and how much it costs, exactly,
to keep our faces from coming apart,

and what makes us pretend so hard
to be so hard.

                And what if we do decide
to kill each other, to turn this chance to blood,
to undo the one sacred thing?

                        What then? Who's glad?

What's fixed?
With everything to lose, brother—what?

KALAMU YA SALAAM

Just Like a Woman

You know I ain't scared of nothing. Not nothing. Mainly cause I been tried, tested and found true. I been stabbed. I been shot. I ain't never been poisoned but I done slept in the same cell with the most vicious bunch of cut throats in the world, thanks to old cigar smoking Judge Shea who sentenced me to a double dime on accessory to armed robbery. I wasn't armed but I was there when we stuck that store up when Peety popped the dude upside the head with the gun, I just stepped politely over the blood and tears flowing on the floor, and went on about my business of rahzooing the cash register. We had sense enough to shoot out the video camera eye, but not sense enough to take the video tape before we left. Aw well, you know, you live and learn. Time ain't nothing but a classroom, and either you learn and move on, or you stay stupid and just keep doing time. I did a dime and loose change behind some stupid shit.

You know the joint is good for getting your head together. It didn't take me long to realize that sticking up poor people was both stupid and evil. First they ain't got nothing much and second why take anything from somebody who ain't got next to nothing? You hear what I'm saying? I view the joint just like grade school, you do that shit once and you ain't never supposed to return. Me, myself, I ain't never going back to the joint, twelve years is a motherfucking Ph. motherfucking D. Besides them young thugs what's showing up now in the slams is straight out ignorant ass fools, you know what I mean?

As I look round this funky ass hole in the wall, it seems to me that everybody in this motherfucker done been up on the yard except for that pretty boy sitting over there checking out every hard leg what walk up in here I guess he know how long he would last in the joint, and then again, some of them living better in prison than they ever could live out here in the world cause there ain't no big time faking and fronting in the joint. Damn near everybody is either sticking and getting sucked or else sucking and getting stuck, so, you know, you kind of get used to men being women. Dudes like pretty boy is a prize that brothers fight and die over everyday. Lil dude like him get a big time murderer to be his old man, yaknow, a cat who got more time than Methusaleem, or whatever that old dude in the bible was called, anyway, they get sponsored by one of them kind of dudes who ain't gon never see the sun shine again.

Being in the joint is just like anything else after you get used to it, it becomes your life. The joint be your life just like being in the world is somebody else's life. You do what you got to do to live. And you do whatever you can do to enjoy your life, you know what I'm saying? At first it be different, but after you spend a bunch of years doing it with dudes, you get used to it. Some people don't, but most people do. It ain't no big thing, not like it seem . . .

Well ain't this a bitch here come Popeye Henry. How in the fuck did he get out? And who that woman he got with him? She look too fine to be Popeye's squeeze. She must be a whore and he must be buying his first piece since getting out. The motherfucker acting like he don't know nobody, strutting around with that real pussy by his side.

"You want another beer?"

"Yeah, give me another one."

"We don't give nobody shit around here. You can buy another one."

"I got money, motherfucker . . ."

"Man, have some respect for your mama. Call me Mr. Motherfucker."

Me and Euclid the bartender been going at it for over two hours now. Euclid's a funny ass motherfucker. He claim he got his name cause he was conceived in the back seat of a Ford when his mama was in high school and she opened up a book that was on the floor and picked the first name she saw. Ain't that some shit?

You don't talk much, do you. You ain't said a word since we been sitting here.

Aw shit, now look at this. Look like Popeye and that broad got some kind of major static happening.

". . . I can say whatever I want to say."

"See how much you can say with a fist all up in your big ass mouth."

Oh Popeye, that ain't no way to treat a lady. Boy, you know I taught you better than that. "Henry, my man, why don't you cool it." She must not be no whore he just met, cause I don't believe he giving her enough money to take a ass whipping like that.

"Who that dipping they lip in my business." Look at him fronting. He ain't even so much as looked over here to see who it is sounding on him. Reaching his hand up in his coat like he packing and I'm supposed to be scared or something.

"It don't matter who it is, right is right, and right ain't never wronged nobody. Just cause you got a beef with your lady, you ain't got to go upside her head."

"Fuck all that shit. A man take care a business wherever the business is."

Now where this motherfucker get off challenging somebody's manhood. See, before I went to the joint I would have been all over that nigga talking that murder mouth shit. But like I told you, I don't plan on going back, and seeing as how I'm still on parole, I don't need to be getting into no fight behind somebody else funny business. Except, you know, I know this nigga. We did time together up on the yard. I know him in ways he don't want nobody to know. Maybe he didn't recognize my voice.

Now look at this shit. He hitting her again just to show me he can hit on a woman. Hey, man watch my back. I don't want no heat slipping up on me while I'm dealing with this roach ass nigga.

"Miss, you ok?"

"Steve, this ain't your business man."

So, you did recognize me. You just fronting but I got something for your fronting ass.

I look at the woman, and she don't say nothing. "I said, are you ok, lady."

"Hey man . . ."

"I'm talking to the lady, Henry. Not to you."

"Yeah, but that lady is with me."

"Meaning?"

"Meaning, this ain't none of your business."

"I'm alright," she finally says cutting the silence of me and Popeye squaring off like some typical Saturday night, two dudes fighting over a bitch shit.

I can hear the place get quiet. There's always this silence before some shit jump off, sometimes the silence is less than a second, sometimes it be a minute or two, but there's always this point where it could go any which way, and it's like everybody be holding their breath. And waiting. The dangerous quiet. That's when you got to act fast.

Popeye slips his hand back in his pocket. Knowing this nigga, I'm sure he got a shank, might even be packing a piece. I turn my attention away from him, hoping to cool the scene out, "What's your name, baby?"

She looks at Popeye when I ask her that. "I'm Marlene."

Popeye glares at her. "What difference it make to you what her name is?"

Look at this motherfucker fronting. "My name is Steve. Me and Henry go back a long ways. We did time together. Did you tell her about me, Popeye?"

"She know I did time. I'm just saying that was then, this here shit is now. And I don't appreciate . . ." I watch him make exaggerated hand motions in his pocket. ". . . you butting into my business."

"When you got out?"

He don't answer me. After we exchange snake eyes for a minute or two, I let it drop and head back to my seat. From over my shoulder I hear the ruckus. "What the fuck you looking at him for, bitch?" And I hear him slap her again. I know Popeye is just acting out on account of he just got out the joint, and he sitting up in here with a bunch of motherfuckers who been up in the joint, so he trying to prove that he's a man and not a turned out, jailhouse bitch, but he ain't got to be beating all over that broad to prove he a man. I can't stand to see no shit like this go down, so I got to do what I got to do.

"Popeye," I say to him as I turn around and walk up in his face. "When you was my woman in the joint, did I treat you this way?"

Henry don't say shit. He kind of shrink back into himself a little, take his empty hand out his pocket, don't say shit, and just walk away straight out the door. Marlene looks confused as a motherfucker.

But, see Popeye should of been cool from the jump and I wouldn't have had to call him out on that mishandling a woman shit. It reflects bad on me for him to act like a thug. Right is right and wrong ain't nothing nice. And, like I said, ain't nothing wrong in doing right cause right ain't never wronged nobody. You know what I mean.

"Hey, Euclid, sell me another beer, motherfucker."

Fireman's Ball

glistening in the heated night glow
yr arced torso radiates

the sculpted bronze intensity
of an earth toned ewe passion mask

yr hypnotic breasts
are brown mesmerizing eyes, yr nipples

dilated pupils aroused into
elongated surprise

yr navel a heavy
nose

flaring
with every sharp breath

& listen
that dark forest, yr sideways mouth

silently chants the sacred syllables
of my secret name

as i plunge into the discovery
of its musky depths

unable to stand
i joyously recline

jumping in the happy immolation
of yr explosive flame

this poem woke me—4:50 A.M.

what most healthily marks
our passage through this whirl
is never stone

neither forged metal
nor mute masonry

nothing that sits
or stands
defiant of time

but rather a quick sensation
potent enough to shape
several generations, e.g.

—the breath
of a baby
well loved
whose own grandchildren also
experience the enabling splendidness
of human touch & caring

a spirit flash which
creates space within us
to pause
& be fed
by the gentle trickle
of ancient rain

every life needs
an inner security system
constantly on,
continuously blinking

sensitively set to alert us
to respond to beauty
regardless of the dawn's shape
or our circumstance thereunder

even if appreciating
means awakening

well before
we are finished

sleeping

EMOTION BROWN

i didn't feel it

i wasn't in the mood
to hear you complain about
why i didn't do this
or didn't do that.
i wasn't down with you
touching me after an
argument, believing that
your intimacy would heal
my pain.
i couldn't get with your
male macho "me man-you woman"
attitude that kept me
confined
insecure
unsure
and faithful . . .
and i ain't tryin' to hear those
silly unspoken words that i
should have transmitted from
your mind with my black woman's
crystal ball.
if you want me to listen . . . then speak.
if you want me to react . . . then ask.
and the last time you loved me
as i lay there
thinking about what i
was going to do the next day,
or tell my girlfriends how pathetic
you've become,

or better yet . . .
go to sleep,
after this melo-traumatic experience.
i realized not only couldn't i dig it.
i didn't feel it.

NADIR LASANA BOMANI

someone's knockin' at my door

movin' from downtown to uptown, from backatown to out frontatown, from that 9th ward to the 10th ward is like traveling from one country to another. although these are just two small separate sections of a strange city named new orleans, their differences are huge like orleans parrish sales taxes.

the first thing I notice when I moved uptown was the arrogant attitude of the big bellied stray cats that strut down flood level sidewalks. stuffed garbage bags saluted from neighborhood curbs without one drop of ammonia on them. where I grew up, downtown, if you didn't baptize your trash bag in some sort of sanctified, chemical concoction before the garbage man passed, your bag would look like a pinata that just got hit by a hurricane. yeah, downtown's homeless kitties would croon in front of your door for any amount of table scraps. but see, uptown, not one feline was meowing at anyone's front step. it was obvious that these animals were being well fed.

almost a week into the new frontatown apartment, me and my pregnant wife were watching a foreign film on video when we heard one of those "who the fuck is that" knocks at the door. i'm not one for surprise visits, so I peeped behind the front screen-less door's curtain to see if it was an overbearing, overanxious, over 40 years of age, future grandparent coming over to unpack & refurbish our lives. instead, there were 2 strange, middle-aged black women on our porch, but they weren't relatives. the darkest lady of the two had some literature stuffed between her right arm. a few obese seconds later I finally saw the title on the front of the papers the lighter-skinned lady was holding: watchtower.

"jehovah fuckin' witnesses," I mumbled to myself, "on a wednesday?!" out backatown, jehovah witnesses invaded houses only on saturdays, but for the most part they had quit the door-2-door sale pitch routine and started cornering people at bus stops. after hearing my mumbled voice the light-skinned witness said to the other one, "did you hear someone?" I pulled back the curtain then shouted, in my most "get from round here voice," "we don't want none!!!" obviously pissed at my straightforwardness & no show on the porch, the witnesses looked at each other, gave an emphatic, "hmph!" then stomped away. there hasn't been a jehovah's witness citing at my front door since.

several months later, mawiyah, my wife, was resting after breast feeding our daughter, nzingha. I was sitting on the edge of the bed watching a chicago bulls game when suddenly, another rare, "who the fuck is that" knock came from the front door. I pulled back the curtain only to find a dingy looking black woman, in her late twenties, staring through my front door's glass window. she had a poorly dressed boy welded to her hip. "excuse me, mista . . . mista . .," she started slurring, "can I speak to you for a sec . . ?" the troublesome expression on the little boy's face literally made my reluctant hands open the door. "can I help you?" I asked through the crack of my still chained door. she began to talk in a groggy, nasal drawl that i've become familiar with from listening to my crackhead uncle bullshit for loot. she gave me some tired "needin' t'get home" speech. I wasn't sold on the story, but thinking about nzingha had me sympathizing with this kid who looked dazed and had the blues bouncing in his eyes. what if i'm wrong? what if her sentimental charade is true? I excused myself from the door and returned with a few dollars that I gave to the woman. she said, "thank you" and took centepede steps down phillip st. toward annunciation. another 10th ward scenario. ya see in the 9th ward addicts would catch yo coming out the grocery store, not bang on your front door for some fix money. I hope she didn't smoke it all up in one hit. hopefully some of it went to the kid.

yesterday, my grandmother, mama theda, came by to baby-sit nzingha. mawiyah had already gone to work and I was two grilled cheese sandwiches away from jettin' to my job. as I was getting ready to sink my teeth into lunch, mama theda shouted from the bedroom, "someone's at the door!" but I had already heard that one "who the fuck is that" knock. I peeped behind the front door's curtain and saw this short, kinda stocky, 30-somethin' black man in a white t-shirt & camouflage pants. I opened the the door wildly, hoping it would send a subliminal message: "don't start none—won't be none." the brother, unfazed by my theatrics, raced into his memorized speech. he was spittin some shit about how he couldn't read or write and how he needed money to get into the salvation army. then, he offered to clean up the trash around my apartment for a small fee. I dug his old school tactics, offering to work for the loot, but to be honest, the job would've been a lay out for him. as for the supposed trash, it would've taken me roughly five minutes to do it myself. I figured if he's ambitious enough with the door-2-door fiasco, he could make enough money to start his own fuckin' army. back in the "9" people would at least wait til you came out of your house or caught you sittin on your porch before asking to cut your grass. here in the 10th they are heavily into this knock on the front door shit. I told podna no thanks, then shut the door. another classic example of beggars asking nickle & dime earnin' people for quarters.

staying backatown, I had the experience of seeing neighbors stealing out of other neighbors' houses. if one neighbor was out of town for a long stint, you might see some other neighbor secondlinin' into that vacationing neighbor's house for the furniture. this scared me, but it also made me conscious of how lowdown some folks can be. this front door 2 beggin' shit seems to be standard upfrontatown. a standard I refuse to entertain any further. the way things have been poppin off so far up here I figure niggas are too bold to break in your house while you're gone. naw, they'll just break in while you're home. so from now on, if I see somebody at the door I don't recognize, I won't answer. see, back in the 9th ward, the cats on all fours cry out at your front door for the handouts, not the cats who won't stand on their twos. in the 10th, stray animals are eating better than stray humans. I just hope the animals that speak broken english don't think that my house is a huge hefty with lots of shit in it, beggin' to be ravaged. cuz I got somethin' waitin' for they moochin' asses and it ain't no ammonia!

M.L.K.

"Happy Martin Luther King Day, ha!"
He said,
"As far as I'm concerned,
I'm glad the nigger is dead."
He was the Grand Puba of this elite company,
and very surprised when he looked over and saw me.
A sweet brown honey
hired to answer the phone.
Because I represent all black people
I felt in no way alone.
"I'm sorry," he said,
in effort to apologize.
"No problem," I said,
"everybody dies."
One month later,
maybe even two,
a memo came out
the Grand Puba had some serious surgery due.
Cards of endearment were requested that we sign
to wish he wellness,
in speedy time.
I signed everything
and didn't feel strange,
in no way,
for signing each card,
"Get well soon,
M.L.K."

Pinafores

. . . stiff and starched and white, soooo white. . . . hugging your waist. . . . itching your neck. . . . how to sit down. . . . don't spill your chocolate milk on it and don't lose your hair ribbons or your braids will come undone. . . . Aubrey is sitting next to me and I think he wants to kiss me. . . . crowding into a playhouse on a hot, steamy afternoon and Molly urinates in the sandbox and makes. . . . then cries because all the other kids start yelling at her. . . . we make crepe paper flowers and popsicle stick sculptures for mommy. . . . and your crayons melt in the sun. . . . color running, dripping on the concrete. . . . a thick, waxy puddle of color with an oil ring spreading out from it . . . and you touch it. . . . because you're not sure why it happened. . . . lunch always consists of green beans and something else served on plastic platters with sections to prevent your beets from running on your mashed potatoes and making them pink. . . . and you take your naps on little futon mats on the floor, perspiration beads on your small, brown face and your pinafore is crumpled underneath your 4 year old body. . . . and ribbons disappear never to reappear again and there is no explanation to be offered to grandma when she asks you what happened to them. . . .

GLENN JOSHUA

on the morning st. bernard

pullin' up to the stop . . . pullin' up to the stop aw man, god please . . .
let her be there.

basin street and canal. people gettin' on the bus.
a buncha roodipoo hardlegs . . . a coupla old folks and some more
lil kids . . . two lovers . . . and there
there she is up there paying her busfare!

my daydream.
my nightdream.
my sweet drum machine thumpin' my heart in my throat, oh
come on and sit by me! (I move my knapsack
this seats reserved, jack!)

and she does. the bus makes a right turn onto canal headed for
clairborne and i'm captivated by a soft scent
softness, eyes soft.
her hand and fingers unwrap a wine candy
(soft)
i've got to say something this time just "good morning."
intelligent and polite so she can know my intentions pure.
honest, no time to waste . . . gettin' close to cohen's tuxedo shop
at the red light.

I glance her way. she's reading toni morrison while sucking on
watermelon flavored contentment, like the weeks i've felt since I
first saw her. she is beautiful and black and smells so doggone good
a mcdonough 35 senior I could tongue kiss till my lips explode
but I hesitate and hold still.

the bus nears kerlerec street and I know what that means:
say something . . . tell her something, fool!
(the bus starts to stop) anything . . . (slower)
she begins to collect her things.
"you're sitting on my coat," she tells me
"oh . . ." I reply. "sorry."
she glances at the sticker taped on my three-ring binder.
"st. augustine? I guess you are sorry . . ."

the bus door opens. she's gone and I turn to look out the window.
she's walking up the street, but not before looking back to the bus,
searching until she finds me. giving a sweet smile that immediately
releases all butterflies, daydreams and desires as if flung
from a slingshot.

I return the smile with a waving finger and she knows
i'll get a chance for
my rebuttal tomorrow.

because i've got her schedule down pat:
the morning st. bernard complete with wine candies,
good reading and cherry chocolate delights in eyes soft . . .
so soft. . . .

next day the bus pullin' up to basin street and canal.

"naw, naw, man! I ain't movin' my knapsack . . .
this seat's reserved, jack!"

KALAMU YA SALAAM

the past predicts the future
(for narvalee)

when you get closer to yr relatives
you will be surprised

at how black they are,
they feel

the fit and familiarity of their emotions in the twilight
how much of your pain they understand
with a knowing smile, and how much of their pain
you never knew, thus you frown
embarassed by your ignorance
and turn to yester-world
altared on the mantle piece:

ancestral photographs, amazingly graceful figures
whose dominant features are boldly ironic eyes
which seemingly float effortlessly just above the surface
of the cream colored paper, inscriptions in unfading black ink
on the reverse "me & shane, dec. 1934"

a small, soft purple, velvet box enshrining a plain gold ring
a slip of torn paper from another era unthrown-away
seven quickly scribbled numerals, the abacadabra key
to a birth, a midnight move to another town, or even
a pledge cut short by accidental death, "oh, it's just a number,"
the slow, quiet response to your investigation

so you pick up a pencil gilded with the name of a 1947 religious
convention attended and delicately place it down beside
an 87 year old hand mirror (you resist the impulse
to look at your reflection, afraid that you might see
unfulfilled family aspirations), this mirror is atop
a piece of lace, pressed, folded, ancient matriarchal adornment

you will be surprised to learn,
as the years go on, everything
your people say sounds like something
from your life story, something
you wondered about sitting in the car
the other day in the hospital parking lot before the visit,
before the treatment

especially if you are intelligent
paid more than $10 an hour
carry credit cards rather than cash
and climb aboard a flying machine more than three times a year

you will be surprised that although you live in some other city
there is a spot with your familial name
blind embossed and hand engraved in the heart-home
of people you seldom see, surprised
that much of your life had already been accurately predicted
by an aunt who knew you before you were born, i.e.

when your mother
and father were courting, staying out later than curfew
and clutching dreams tightly in the naked embrace
of yr conception

JAS. MARDIS

South of Eden
For Rose

Sometimes,
 I have to be reminded
So, the rain comes flashing through
    pouring life from on high
  where the clouds have grown gray and fat
with what someone once said were,
   "The tears of the devil's wife"
  who was being spanked

    and I'm reminded
when all is done
  by how glorious and green the world turns
 after being drenched and drained of its dullness
by the rain

  and I'm reminded
 by the copious pages of grasses turned again
       toward the verdant sheets of green
 stretching ever so fully
   'cross the fields and vacant lots
  forever sprouting skyward into the heads of the trees
   sliding with elegance into the valleys and
 over the hills
    then climbing the ivy against the walls of lattice work and brick
and window trim

and I'm reminded
    by how clear and blue and calm
the rain turns the sky
 of how sacredly calm the earth's beauty
can pulse the human blood
        and excite the body toward passions long forgotten
    of how one simple gaze of
                grasses and tree tops turned back to green
      and leaves reclaiming their reds and yellows
and the beige and white of buildings pulling up from the ground
  the ground churning the brown dust and dirt and earth
        into a thing of beauty
   like the wide eyes of a woman ready to love
        and I'm reminded
   by the early morning/late evening smells of that dirt
that earth sectioned off by garden fences

   that earth
  peeled back against itself into the frenzy of a mound
that earth
   and the smell of it all
 streaking through the air and finding the nostrils
   sparking the heart and the memory
 reminding
    me to never forget the early mornings of my youth
    when the open window brought me this same
 fresh-earth aroma

   and awoke me to it
so that I'd stumble to that window and look out
 into my mother's garden

with the tall, green stems bending under the tomato's growth
while swollen stalks of okra and peas watered the mouth
and branches of pecans and plums and persimmons
rallied their growth against our crunch of apple-pears
in their shade

and watermelons burst under the force of their juices

and sometimes I need to be reminded
that I am south of Eden
with her garden growing dense with promise and remembrances

and I open my mind's eye to the beauty of it all
and make a wish on never forgetting to know
something this wonderful
is just a rain away

Invisible Man

Too often
the sun rises and retreats
and I am no one
not even me

and the world's eyes
pass through me   over me
and the heavy shouldered walking
that I do
and the swagger in my steps
doesn't matter
doesn't matter
and the rise of air in my chest
and the full barrel of my chest
doesn't matter

and the heavy fisted pounding
of my words and ideas and feelings
doesn't matter
doesn't matter
and the hurried shouting of my blood
through my veins
through my veins
doesn't matter
and the jagged resolve of my anger
the constant checking of my anger

and the constant/steady checking
of my angers
doesn't matter

and the, and the, and the
sadness of my life
the daily sad nest of my life
being seen
being looked upon and not seen
or heard
or had
or noticed
beyond anything
other than being in the way
being seen
only to be avoided
only to be watched
only to be ignored
replaced
dismissed
Dis—
Dis—
Dis—

I never read Ellison's "Invisible Man"
or Wright's "Black Boy"
or John Howard Griffin
and his "Black Like Me"
as anything more
than
life guides
because I knew long ago
somewhere
in the womb
where the wall of blood
and birth mucus flowed

I knew
while floating in that sack
  that swollen sanctuary
I knew
   even then
  with that tiny hole of daylight
calling me
  I knew then—even then

as I churned into becoming a child
  as I swelled my mother's womb
and pushed her belly outward
 into the round pleasure
  that pregnancy brings the world

  I knew then
 that
as far as the world was concerned
 I was making
  my most visible
   mark

Sting

for James Ward Lee

Sometime
the smell of lemon
on my hands

reminds me of my father
and of being home
for the last time

the swollen acrid smell
of lemons

and the remembered yellow skin
with its pimples gone awry
dotting the landscape and

chasing the perfect oval
hull
covering all that is possible
to cover
in that seasonal lifetime
of a lemon
dotting the rise and sloping fall
of a hull:

Yellow to yellow-dotted black aromatic pore
seeping out the blinding
mellow
quick, sharp breaths
of this lemon life
a season of smelling
and tarting the tastes of things:

Like water into thirst quenching 'ades
          fish from bland sea palate
          into a chasing, feverish rush
    of once fighting muscle
        pulling tightly against the line
        making this plate
    of bones and baked flesh
again
worth the swollen chest
        of its being here

  lemon
the squeaky run of its juice
    over my hands
          fingers

  chasing tightly into the
smallest cut

          into the hell of broken flesh
        into the naked wounds
of being
          home
    for the last time

Home Home Home
    sometimes
  the worst of the four lettered
          words

  Home
for the last time

    with my father's breath
  packed and ready to go

leaving his heaving
    hairy chest
   beneath his sweat soaked
    death shirt

   home
like his last words
  "lemonade" & "son"

    home
  running over me
  there—
    here—
with these lemons

   bursting under my grip
spilling
  exploding
  crying the hot juice
 of giving in

   like my father
  who
wanted lemonade
  as his last
  throat quenching drink

 So he asked me
   to make it

 and now
  the smell of lemon
     on my hands

will mean
always
    that his throat is dry
  in a room
that's just a sting
    and a step away

PERFORMERS

Featured here are excerpts from two plays by sharon bridgforth, whose stories are shaped by memories of the southern wy'mn and men who raised her. She says:

i still hear their voices/see their faces/remember how they made a room feel/these beautiful, resilient people/some still here/some passed on/ some i've only known in dreams are now me.

i believe that when we/people of African descent blend inflection/ into nation/and movement to make words say what we mean, we are actually participating in ancient ritual the blood memory that music-dance-visual art-drama are literal aspects of
Prayer
power
NOMMO (Life force)

this is the way we conjure
a roll of the neck/snap of the fingers   a pause
when we raise and lower our voices/with whirling bodies and hand gestures
we change the space around us/invoke Ancestors, Orishas and Saints
we make language/talk.

for me/once i realized that my work-words were for performance once i discovered theatre, i knew i couldn't do it the european way/i knew we'd need a non-linear space to invite the Spirits to move in.
i feel my job as writer/artistic director for THE ROOT WY'MN THEATRE COMPANY is to remember
to listen
to tell my grandmother's stories/as i tell mine,
and to acknowledge that what i'm really doing is
Praying.

sharon bridgforth

LOVVE/RITUALS & RAGE[1]

"lovve/rituals & rage" is the telling of one soul's journey through many Life-times, stealing-a-way/making a way outta no-way and dying for those to come it's about lovve re-cycling, Ancient Truths and generational binding. the stage is an altar Honoring Yemaya (Orisha of the Moon/Ocean/Waters of wy'mn). there are four performers each representing an element (Earth, Wind, Fire, Water). the performers, who never leave the stage, create sound and visual environment when not speaking (canned music should not be used during the performance).
ROOTN ME is Water, she is an old Soul trying to learn to balance her nurturing Spirit's/giving and receiving.
GLORY ME is Fire, trying to learn to balance will and desire.
MANY ME is Earth, she is a young Soul/closest to The Spirit/she is witness trying to balance other people's pain and her own heart's joy.
MILLENNIA ME is Air, she is the Original Soul that the others generate from/she is trying to gather the pieces of herself/she tells the story as witness-calling and protecting through dance/she rarely speaks but is always present.

---

[1]THE ROOT WY'MN THEATRE COMPANY performance piece"lovve/rituals & rage" premiered in 1993 at The Vortex Theatre in Austin, Texas /kicking off THE ROOT WY'MN THEATRE COMPANY's first tour. The original touring party included: Arriama Matlock-Abdula as ROOTN ME, Kaci Fannin as GLORY ME, Anoa Monsho as MILLENNIA ME, and Sonja Parks as MANY ME. Sculptor Marsha Gomez contributed set design/art and the concept of stage-as-altar that ROOT WY'MN still use. With Michelle Parkerson as director/consultant in bringing "lovve/rituals & rage" to Life ROOT WY'MN created a collaborative Work spun out of text/company vision/and the bodies & Spirits of all involved. Blocking/vocalizations/movement and interpretation of the script came as a result of honoring the process of working together and celebrating community & sista hood. ©sharon bridgforth.

lovve/rituals & rage

(Start in black, performers enter from audience/walk-up various aisles chanting, "when they came i was drumming." Once on stage lights fade up as ROOTN ME, MANY ME and GLORY ME pour water, light candles and pray at the altar while MILLENNIA ME begins cleansing the space with dance and sage. MILLENNIA ME blesses stage/invokes spirits of peace and harmony, pays tribute to and calls down guardian ancestors/she ends on knees, head and arms raised in praise.)

(Lights out.)

(Slowly fade up dream-tinted lighting/the stage should have an airy fluid appearance/MANY ME has taken MILLENNIA ME's place on knees.)

MILLENNIA ME:
this is my story.
i am the first thought without
words am all language uttering
motion/i am rhythm
moving beyond time was
sung before never/i is
One Wo'mn
bringing
reaching
to return
my story
to me . . .

(MILLENNIA ME repeats her story/this time many me says the lines with her backwards.)

ROOTN ME:

i grew up n da woods
fak/our houz waz so fa bak
dem parts didn hab no nam
so we calln it
way-bak/dats where i grew up/yeah
in way-bak, lousyanna.

my ma'ma's people waz full-blood Koromanteen
from Kromantine on da Gold Coast,
bought
ova slaves/da
Koromanteens
escap'd
inta da hilly-woods
made a way
nexta da Arawak/who
waz-first-on-dat-land.
white folk didn neva see da Kromantine
no mo
dat scar'd em/yeah/white folk
said da Koromanteen turn'd theyselves inta
bush n tree/say dats why na n den
a bush o tree wou raise up
n kill sheself a white folk.
ma'ma always laugf bout dat say,
glory me says with rootn me
"gurl, dat go ta sh'w ya dem backra dun't nu
nuthn
kep em scar'd/kep we safe!"

GLORY ME:
na/my paw'paw's people
waz all-bloods-mix'd/made he be geecheee.
he mak a livn readn shells
by da port   till he met my ma'ma
who stepn off da boat from da hilly-woods/lookn

fa hope.
paw'paw say ma'ma tooka hold of him eyes n next
thang he know'd he donn jump'd da broom n waz
livn in way-bak

na/paw'paw mak lik ma'ma spell'd him/i don't
know/but i know
paw'paw be smiln
all da time

till one day paw'paw wenta town
neva come back.

MANY ME:
he stopn a white man from tryn ta take a cul'lad
gurl-child's-wo'mnhood by force/paw'paw beat
dat white man/who tole da deputy/n da sheriff
n a-whole-crowd-of-white peoples/took my
po black/red/high-brown paw n burn'd him
alive n da town square/spitn at him n calln him
out his nam.

my ma'ma saw it all in her dreams/said
paw'paw he com'n ta her be moan'n
said she had ta go be wid him/said
not ta worry
she'd
be
right
bak/i
thank ma'ma went in dem
woods n gavn sheself
ta death.

ROOTN ME:

na/but she did come bak
i waz rais'd by Spirits/yeah!
right dere in way-bak lousyanna
dey rais'd me/ma'ma
paw'paw and dey peoples.
only thang bout it, i neva figur what me
nam be dey
all been calln me somethang deffrent in
deffrent languages/cept
ma'ma who calln me "baby
    all (done in a rondo)
    baby/she whoz sangn calls da Spirits down
    baby/she who is Wind
    baby/the trees lovve her
    baby daughta"

GLORY ME:
n paw'paw who not calln me nuthn cause all he do
is moan
ma'ma say he still mad at da white
folk/say anga donn tied him tongue.
na/mus be a great numba wid dem tongue tied
cause i donn hearn a whole-lota moan'n in my dey/yeah.

ROOTN ME:
na/well anyway
i nam'n myself baby may-fine
cause one day ma'ma's
baby may-fine
lovve.
i sho be lookn
i even goes ta da port/watch dey come off da
boats/i be lookn/i say
fo somebody ta LOVVE me wid all dey
heart/somebody i wouldn mind die'n fo

and spendn all-time wid.

(repeat "baby" rondo up with marching/from different areas of the stage
they come center/steppn building to a crescendo/this is a warrior-wy'mn-
celebration a bringing forth and claiming of power/a syncopated act of
bonding/the march continues faintly under the following)

MANY ME:
here dey came.
gre-gre gurls/from dere
crossn ova wid
fury dey
comn dwn da road
stirn dust
da sound of feet clappn
Earth/n laugfta
go befo dey.

all who got sense
git in da house
n hide behin peekn
watch gre-gre gurls
comn/carryn
somebody
da blues.

(end of march)

MANY ME:
last time dey
come from dere
i got rustled
up in dey tracks/whirldround
misray and strife   i
found myself
middle some-whole-lotta

somethang.

didn even know
dey from nuthn
cept
befo waz a time
long time
i lovve dem each

thats why i could
ramba amongst dey,
live ta tell it.

dere was
gre-gre/long-gone-come
back fo mo
and her gurls,
done-donn
  soon-come/and
    she.

first time i saw dey again
done-donn
waz standn
in a pool of blood

standn
ova somebody
had tried
ta take her dady's land/her
waz standn

(the following needs to include a choreographed move that will appear
again)
blade-drippn-blood/butt

waggn/back hunch'd/neck
crankn/head swaggn/hands
on hips
(end of choreographed move)

that gurl waz standn say
"my paw's blood
make dem fields pleny,
dem flowers many-full,

you da one open he wound   kept it
pour'd/so him couldn't neva
git up from dat place
you put he down in

bout time we put
yo blood
in da soil
see what happen!"

chile
i had done seen
enough done-donn,
try ta tip-a-way
no see mo/but
the corner of my eye
look round
saw she,

stalkn
like she sista
cept full/wid-child
stormn like thunda
stomach
big-ole-ball-could-flood

the sea

umph!

furtha-look-round/see
soon-come
lawd/lawd/lawd
her don't say nuthn
don't move
nor utta

jes stare

cold-as-hell-hard-as-ice/cuttn notion stare
move wind   kill dat man/yeah,
him didn die by no blade of done-donn,
soon-come stare the life outta he

jes stare
scare the black
offa my ass/i
got on up from thru dere
neva need know who
what fo
or how long

sh'itt!

i hearn
she
drop her baby right dere on da spot/when
soon-come
caught the chile
done-donn screamn,
glory me
 "paw

paw
ma-paw"

MANY ME:
'parently justice freed dey daddy Spirit/been calln dat baby
ma-paw
ever since.
so-na-see/ma-paw
is da daughta of she
da ma'ma of sista/who is nosey-nappy's ma'ma/and
dey all come from maw black, dem
gre-gre/long-gone-come
back fo mo
and her gurls
done-donn
  soon-come/and
   she/dey
from dere,
crossn ova
bringn
those ta come . . .

(MILLENNIA ME begins to march/the march turns into potion stir-
ring as she dances)

GLORY ME:
this is a lost art you know   a bonding gonn/an act
of lovve not to be knowd any longer.

ROOTN ME:
useta make greens every sunday/i'd git up before the sun and pick em
out big-momma's garden/i was a young thang then. june-bug-miller-
jones useta say i had legs ta die for and enough ass to make a dead man
take notice.

i'd git out in mae-dean's garden
every sunday
boot up
one foot each side the row.
butt swirln to the left/then i'd swirl it to the right
cause thats how you pick greens/yeah.
go down the line
side to side
justa pickn.
and every sunday
ole dirty-dickie say,
"looka here, somebody ova yonda is sho-nuff pickn greens today
thank ya
jesus!
when you gonn let me come ova/and
have some gal?"
every sunday i'd holla back
"when hell freezes ova and every coloured holds a dime/and don't be
thankn the lawd for what the devil done put in yo mind!"

big-momma and her girls and us would git in that kitchen
and have a time.
folk don't realize/but
it wasn't hardly bout eating much as it was bout healing
and loving one the
other.
bertha-mae git to sanging/voice so big
make the walls quake

(the following is from a traditional spiritual/should be sung)
"well, well, well,
every heart needs a fixn
every mind needs a healn
every soul needs a meetn,
well, well, well . . ."
(end of song)

85

GLORY ME:
(bull-jean is a wo'mn-loving-wo'mn not a wo'mn telling a man's story)
cleandra marie la beau
say she lik the way i
tickle her spot/say
folk keepa fiddln round but cain't seem ta
find it/lik i
can she
take my hand place it on her heart/say
thats my spot bull-jean/and since you touch it so sweet
i'm gonn let you see what else of mine you can find ta tickle . . .
oh/i'm so in lovve
till i'm sick/jes
hurt
all ova body
ache
mind
sore
heart
hurt/jes
hurt

and it all began when i looked in the eyes of THAT WO'MN.

me/they call bull-dog-jean
i say thats cause i works lik somekinda ole dog
trying ta git a bone or two
they say it's cause i be sniffn after wy'mns
down-low/begging and thangs

whatever.

one day
i was sitting in my yard
talen tales and dranking wid my pal lou when

i thought i heard a rustling
     i didn't look up cause the dogs was jes
     laying-round-not-saying-a-thang
     usually they barks at everythang
     cluding me
so i jes kepa-dranking and talen
till i heard a voice
     "hello"
well i lik ta fell ova in the petunias
     sounded lik heaven ta me
i looked round and lawdy-mercy what i have ta do that fo
     na/i know you done heard this befo
but this wo'mn is here to testify: DON'T MESS WID THEM
FULL-GROWN/FULL-FLEDGE/SHO-NUFF-HOT-BUTT
WY'MNS!
they'll drop a spell on you quicker'n you can say please
chile
i looked up and SHE caught me
wid her eyes/i ain't got loose yet.

fo the longest i didn't even see the rest of her
so lost in them eyes/deep
clear/flicker'n brown/spirit-talking eyes
     take me now lawd i said
     fo one moment in them eyes and i done lived full-in-yo glory
cain't recall much was said right away
too busy staring in them eyes.
fo the longest i didn't even see the rest of her

then i saw lips/full and quick to smile
     loose me lawd/git me out her spell,
     i said/mouth watering/i thought,
     bet she sho know how to do some
     good loving/lips so fine and all.
fo the longest i didn't even see the rest of her

then i looked on down and saw nipples lunging/hips ready ta roll
    sweet glory in the morning
    i'm done seen an angel
    in the form of flesh
thats when i gave up the ghost
jes said
here,
fo i know'd SHE was the kinda wo'mn make you want ta give it up/say
baby
  take me
    take all i got
      take all i'll ever git
        tell me
          what you want gal
here
        i'll give it jes ta see you smile.

fate were before me
giving me a big brown hello.

and sho-nuff
i done spent all the rest of my days
tickln a permanent smile on that wo'mn's face.

GLORY ME:
(as GLORY ME sings "bull-jean's song"she should engage audience
as if she is a club singer)
baby, baby,
baby please don't go
you give me the blues
so sweet and low

baby, baby,
baby please don't go
gottdamn gal

i loves you so

i'll give you my heart
you got my mind in tow
i'll pawn my spirit
just say you ain't gonn go

you honorary and mean
don't come home most nights
you know you like ta holla
like ta fuss and fight

but please don't leave
baby, please don't go
i don't know why i love you so
cept you give me the blues so sweet and low

baby, baby
baby please don't go
gottdamn gal
you know i loves you so!

all
(we transition into another time perhaps the '50's during the "migration" of southern Blacks west "bull-jean's song" leads into a short "doo-
wap" which becomes the following song)
i want a
  root slaying
    potion swaying
      rump whirling
        attitude laying

big-bangie-ass
sista ta
serve it up/throw it down/give
to me

ethno-colour
heat

i want an
urban afrodite/a
cornbread fed Oshun lead
Black queen/ta
raise up on me
and Work

i want
  i want
    i say i want
a Black wo'mn!

(we are now at "the b.y.o." GLORY ME is bull-jean and ROOTN ME
is her buddy jucey la bloom, there is no interaction or acknowledgment
between MANY ME and the other players)

MANY ME:
i knew
trouble had done leftwhen i saw
bull-jean sittn at the b.y.o. with
jucey la bloom/i knew
trouble was gonn

cause jucey don't drank
and bull-jean don't hang
lessn some wo'mn done broke she heart/and baby
bull-jean musta sho-nuff been hurtn
cause jucey had done drank the fat part of a rat's ass jigg'ed.
you see bull-jean and jucey la bloom
friends from last-Life/they so close
they feel one-the-other's pain
jucey say

ROOTN ME:
i thank
i'll begin life again/come back
a dog/cock my leg or squat bow-wow-mafucka,
folk gonn haveta deal wid MY shit
next time round!

MANY ME:
yesur/they business jes schooch-ova ta my table cause you know
i ain't a nosey-wo'mn

ROOTN ME:
she ain't nuthn but a periodic-ho,
ain't even got sense nough ta charge on a regular basis

MANY ME:
bull-jean sit
holdn she head
low ta the table stream-a-tears
rolln down the left side she face/her
don't bat a eye/nor make sound.
jucey, on the other hand
jesa howln/rockn backwards and forwards/eyes rolln

ROOTN ME:
(doing the above mentioned action)
why/bull-jean/why you git we in this mess gurl
why?

(ROOTN ME stays seated/holdn her head, MILLENNIA ME dances/
her movements are very sensuous/done to entice and capture)

GLORY ME:
trouble/came in
stood to the side,
  made me

sense her first
russln skirt/jiggln jewelry/clickn
heels   trouble/came in
smelt like sunshine   like
freedom on a bed of poses/trouble
made me want her
before i ever saw her face   she
entered my heart
and held me/trouble
came in ass poppn
from side to side
she carried me across the room in her gaze/i
got lost
haven't found my way back
from trouble/she holds me
in her smile   i fit
between the moist on her lips/i
fit between her ears/i fit
in the middle of her intent/i fit
at the end of her fingers
i fit
in the pressure of her voice/her
heat as it lifts me/at the tip
of her thoughts as they extend themselves/with
the extent of her desire/i
fit   i donn layed down with trouble/and
cain't
git
up!

trouble came in,
  stood to the side
    and took me
home.

(during the following jazz song GLORY ME joins MILLENNIA ME
and we see her "captured")

ROOTN ME and MANY ME:
come to me   with
both arms/come
seek me
and dream
come willing
to let me find you
free of the past
sober
and filled with desire
come to me/open
and let me
get to
you.

MANY ME:
this is
my story/i am pieces
of myself keeping
time
over and
over i   no longer know
it all/my story
i try to find
myself but
cannot.

sorrow/unclaimed
memories and my own image
haunt me/i
don't know why
screaming

screaming
    screaming/pain.

this is
my story
and i am waiting
to hear it/myself . . .

(the following is jazz. the characters should sometimes overlap their
lines, sometimes stagger starting/should vary the rhythm of delivery
taking on various sounds, i.e. scatting, be-bop, horns and maddness. by
the end of this piece the characters begin to cross over find and become
each other)

GLORY ME:
home.
riding
the edge of maddness
i sit/tight   close
to the reality that though i
contemplate options

i have
not
one
choice . . .

MANY ME:
home.
i gave voice to need
intoned destiny/with desire
called her/down/with
song
made her
know
it was time to come

home
it was my voice that lead her back
and caused her
to know/glory
sweet-glory
was her name
and it was i that rhythmed her return/i
dream of moving thru the rivers that flow between us   of
riding/tides
till our currents connect/i dream
of dancing thru the storms that bind us
of whirling winds and passion
of your voice settling in my ear/like a song
i dream of stroking your melody
of playing you like a finely tuned instrument/i dream
millennia me
of taking you

in my dreams
the rivers
that flow
between us
carry the taste
of you
to me/i
to you
from
many lives before/i
dream of you
and me
and
the moonlight
crossing over
again
  and
    again

and
   again.

GLORY ME:
i am trouble's child
descendant of grief/i been
fucked by sorrow
and left without hope/i
am saddness
running i with excess

the last time
lovve-called-me-home
i was NOT into
giving/reconciling or
being available

love will NOT
loosen memories/unfold
pain/mix-regrets
with pleasure/or render
me silent   i said
so
the last time
lovve-called-me-home
i ran
quietly
away.

ROOTN ME:
home
is where greens are cooking
the choir sings
the booty shakes
blood boils
and the tasting

is sweet/home is
me/in
you/singing
   glory
   sweet
glory
come back
home
to me.

GLORY ME:
i entered
running
with trouble/with maddness/with
fear
with threats/i
ran
past the liquor store/the
soul food restaurant/the
boarded up record store/past
the tore-down fence/the alley/the
motel/the bar
past the men leering
round corners and
paper bags/thru
the exhaust of passing cars
i ran
past strangers
too busy to notice
a girl running at
dusk on friday/i ran
because
at thirteen
my body betrayed me
began to bleed
 from quiet places/announced

my presence
with its flow/made me
a living target

(to defend herself GLORY ME does the blade dance that MANY ME
did earlier/during the gre-gre gurls story/except this time it has a fren-
zied-maddened edge to it MILLENNIA ME does martial arts defense/
fighting motions that include audible breathing techniques)

    those who wanted
    to touch the moon
      and could not
    decided to chase me instead
i rushed down the streets where
anguish ruptured vision
and marred hope's path
    i'm gonn fuck you
    in that dumpster
    you breathless bitch /i
am trouble's child
    running with fear.

(lights out abruptly/in the black we her MILLENNIA ME complete
her fighting moves-her breath is the last thing we hear/wait a few beats
before lights up on the next scene)

ROOTN ME:
home.
they filled
the room
with laughter
hot-sauce-craklin-pig-skins
and bid wisk.
they filled the room

with bourbon
ester lauder

MANY ME:
and Aretha/baby
baby sweet
baby
they filled the room
bosom/rocking
hips/heated hearts and
laughter/they
filled the room

GLORY ME:
with hugs
and lipstick
smooching cheeks/they
  smiled at me
with smothered porkchops
greens and rice/and
"i heard it through the grapevine"
from velvet chairs
next to large lamps
neath velvet pictures
where they
played games with male visitors/and
i don't remember
what they said/i
remember
that they filled the room and
smiled at me
rootn/many and glory me
and i have since
been searching
for wy'mn to
smile at me

and fill
my room.
glory
this is
my story not every wo'mn/is
One Wo'mn
coming round
telln/i
giving birth to me/glimpsing
grasping Life come back/we
One Wo'mn
dere is many others/but
dis is my story/i
crossn ova
returnn us-self to we/many
time long time
from na
i be telln my story to me . . .
all One Wo'mn/together like a spoken word chorus
i been
soul-cycling
  heart-hopping
    and image returning
i have seen my
memory in the eyes
of strangers/i been waiting
a long time/want to smile
let me
smile
at you girl/i
want to
come
home   inside/you
where i need to be/you
in an unnamable way
feel like

home
to me/i
want
to
come/please
call me home now
love

MILLENNIA ME:
glory
  sweet
glory

GLORY ME:
call my name
and
i WILL
come.

MILLENNIA ME:
my womb
is a cushion/still
warm from having
held you/my
womb
is round   still
thick from accommodation
my womb is fertile
still
from you presence/my
womb is
empty
glory
sweet
glory
come

back
home
to me.

all
this
is
my
story.
unremembered memories/of fragmented
me revealing myself to we
finding
us in
deep voice/tipsy church
amen/uh-huh
yonda/juke joint
and mooshine understanding
potlicka
hamhocks/sista
daughter's gurl
and altars   lovving
big-butt
candy ass/honey
bustn/spell throwing/hip-shakn me
calln me home

this is my story,
i am the first thought without
words am all language uttering
motion/i am rhythm
moving beyond time was
sung before never/i is
One Wo'mn
bringing
reaching
to return

my story
to me!

(lights out)

the end

dyke/warrior-prayers[1]

i don't know
how
i ended up
on my back
  but i did
i heard myself
  just say no
declined
the offer/with a smile
said
lets have tea instead
  but somehow
i ended up
on my back
  again   looking
at a
done
been
quit-wo'mn
grinning
down at me.

i'm fi'nta
get up though.

ain't gonn
let you
lay-up in my mind/know'n
you won't stay   can't have
no
aura rubn/breath suckn/stroke
my Spirit without commitment
you

are fooln with
God's intentions
between us/so
i'm fi'nta get up
for good
  soon
i'm tired of
distract-me-can't-think
tears/over
you *for now*
        talk softly
        to me.
        open your arms
        and
        say sweetly
        my name
        hold
        my loneliness away/come on
        and
          move me
        until the pain
        you left
        in my
        Heart
        is gonn . . .

the glide the stride
  the hips the eyes
    sway-swirln
      memories that
        can't be denied
i'm caught
in an undone ritual
from last-Life's blues/i am
still
trying to survive/you

need to know
that wasting
time is a sin/and
i been sinning
dreaming
a temporary love
stay.
i got all
these drums and thangs
off in my head
and i may not understand
how i keep ending up
on my back
for you/but
i
know
that each time you
come
you
leave/with
a little piece
of my mind
which means you
are counter
to the evolution
of my
revolution
  cause i needs all my mind

since i can't mobilize my thoughts
with you/you
must
go
cause
to love me
  is revolutionary

      to love me is revolutionary
       it is
        revolutionary
          to
            love
              me/it is
orbital motion   it is
political seizure/it is
momentous mufuckn change/wake up
walk-out
  sit-in
    boycott
     and
ride
  to
    freedom on a
premeditated deliberation of the dismantling of
this swine-funky-ass
still-racist-system

to love
me
is
revolutionary

I
am
the child
of the daughter of a
just-waxed-Moon gurrl who
birthed the African
that jumped ship
and flew back home
to seek him Ancestors
guard his seed/destined
to walk through

the door of no return
into
the arms of slavery/i am
the gran-granny's/daughter
of the wo'mn ·
guided
to the Indigenous Chief that
took her people in to safety/i have
blood memories of
the Red Road '
and
the African Way
  i can hear the drum
but can't
recall
the chant/i
no longer know
the cry of names
that proceeded me/i
am
trying to remember
        Harriet Tubman
        Frederick Douglass
i am trying
        Old Gran Nanny
        Black Elk
to remember
        Tituba
        Marie Laveau
i am trying
        Martin Luther King
        Malcom X

to remember
        Huey Newton
        Caesar Chavez

i am listening
>Langston Hughes
>Audre Lorde
and
Praying
>Yemonja
>Tequantla
>Mother of God
>Keeper of the Waters of Life
>OH MIGHTY AND DIVINE GUARDIAN SPIRITS
>WHO'VE GONE BEFORE
>WHO PAVED THE WAY
>WHO BLESS US NOW
have mercy
>HOLY AND SACRED ONES
protect us and lead the way
i am

WE
sitting in the Sun
waiting for the Moon
to come back
and carry
Us
Home.
i am
standing
firm-footed
in the Blood of my people

i got all these drums and thangs
off in my head
and
i may not
understand
how

i keep ending up
on my back
for you/but
i know
that each time you
come
you leave/with
a little piece
of mind
which means you
are counter
to the evolution
of my revolution
  cause i needs all my mind
so eventually
i will
get off my back
and
STAND
eye to eye
with you
before
i turn
and
walk away!

[1]*dyke/warrior-prayers* is about being a contemporary/Ancestral hearing gurrl/it is a
look at the disfigured image of a wo'mn trying to survive the cycle of cultural abuse/
imposed by a society built on blood. "dyke/warrior-prayers" asks how can you find
Hope in the face of hate & how can a tortured Soul hear its own yearnings. the excerpt
comes towards the end of the show, giving evidence of the character's Ancestral hearing, Spiritual yearning, shedding and deliverance to Calling. . . . THE ROOT WY'MN
THEATRE COMPANY performance piece copyright 1996 by sharon bridgforth. Cau-
tion: Professionals and amateurs are hereby warned that *dyke/warrior-prayers* is subject to a royalty and is fully protected under the copyright laws of the United States,
and of all countries covered by the International Copyright Union, the Pan-American
Copyright Convention, and the Universal Copyright Convention. All rights are strictly
reserved. Particular emphasis is laid on the question of readings, permission for which
must be security in writing from: Root Wy'mn Theatre Company, 201 W. Stassney
Suite 502, Austin TX 78745.

TELLERS

In 1926 *The Nation* published dueling essays by Langston Hughes and George S. Schuyler that debated the worth and expanse of "Afamerican" literature, in particular that of southern blacks. Schuyler asserted that the artistic southern black was merely aping his long-time oppressor. At best, the southern black, having long endured an odious caste system, had as much ownership of his *creativity* as any similar peasant class. His contention was that the southern Negro was a foreign cultural article to his northern, West Indian and African brethren.

"True, from dark-skinned sources have come those slave songs based on Protestant hymns and Biblical texts known as the spiritual, work songs and secular songs of sorrow and tough luck known as the blues . . . but these are contributions of a caste in a certain section of the country. . . . They are no more expressive or characteristic of the Negro race than the music and dancing of the Appalachian highlanders or the Dalmatian peasantry are expressive of the Caucasian race."

In his rebuttal, Hughes pays homage to a hypothetical, promising young black poet (I imagine of northern stock) who laments a culturally siphoning, "I want to be a poet—not a Negro poet."

"This young poet's home is, I believe a fairly typical home of the middle class. . . . it would be (difficult) for an artist born in such a home to interest himself in interpreting the beauty of his own people. He is never taught to see that beauty . . . (he is taught) to be ashamed of it . . ." Hughes counters. "Certainly there is, for the American Negro artist who can escape the restrictions the more advanced among his own group would put upon him, a great field of unused material ready for his art. . . . There are the low-down folks, the so-called common element, and they are the majority—may the Lord be praised! They have their nip of gin on Saturday. . . . Their joy runs, bang! into ecstacy. Their religion soars to a shout. . . . They furnish a wealth of colorful, distinctive material for any artist because they still hold their own individuality in the face of American standardizations."

The most recent trend of publishing the *new black writer* brings this pair of essays full circle, although all would agree that the publishing standards are in greater question today than in 1926. The question of whether black writers, from all corners of the compass, are aping the topics, style and overall characteristics of white writers is again at the forefront of the publishing world—or should be. This trend moves from pseudo-abberant female sexuality and black male bashing, to the gang-banging, drug cultured chic of the East and West coasts. Occasionally, as with Oklahoma's Clifton L. Taulbert and the prolific contributions of J. California Cooper, we get a quick glimpse of "black life" in the central states. Otherwise, those interested in "black writing" are awash in, as Schuyler has termed it "lampblacked" versions of the various genres: Romance; Mystery; Essay; Theatre and Fiction. To its compunctious credit, the new black spiritual stands alone in its self-caricaturization as any oppressive scheme could have hoped to create.

Hughes's "The Negro Artist and the Racial Mountain," and Schuyler's "The Negro-Art Hokum," were the impetus for establishing the following section. I hope that you will find these selections original in voice and unique in the shaping of characters. Herein are the tales and folk elements that have long sustained the people and cultures of the southwest region.

JESSE GARFIELD TRUVILLION

A Stray Dog's Great Day

The one story of the Thicket that paints forever for me the beauty and the transcendence of our lives in the midst of the woods, along the streams, in the fields, in the gardens and along the trails was the sojourn with us of a stray dog we named "Rover." My dad sang a song of a dog named Rover who was loved and adored. Perhaps it was that favored song of his that gave us reason to name that stray, unwanted, ugly, mixed breed, mangy and flea carrying dog.

Sometimes a full grown dog was gotten rid of by dropping the poor critter near someone's house. I think, someone you didn't like very much or to someone who really had it coming. The tall, bony, light-gray coated dog with several markings appeared in front of our house. Sick and barely alive he was standing out in the road near the mailbox.

"Don't feed him and he'll leave" was the instruction that my baby sister and I received from my mother. The other children were at school. Modestine and I were too young to go, which was fine with me because we saw him first. That made him ours, or you might say mine, since Modestine already had her a pet calf, Butter Ball. This was a dog and no matter Mother's warnings, I couldn't resist the urge to make him a pet. I first slipped him a biscuit. Soon, he wasn't afraid of me and I got him some bacon. Not long after that Modestine joined in my disobedience and the revitalization of Rover was underway.

After a little while his bones disappeared. As he fattened up he began to wag his tail pretty regularly for me. So we washed him up with no protest from Mother, who we observed passing along some scraps as well. The better he looked the more it seems he was given. Since he was enjoying God's blessing, food from our table, Modestine and I figured that he needed to give due response and become a Christian. Since he was now a part of the family a baptism was in order. So it was that "a gathering" took place at the waterside. It was a lovely meeting and Rover was a willing candidate. We had not known from where he had come or how he had become so poor, but he was one of us now, a stray no longer.

He was baptized in the same stream where Butter Ball was made a Methodist, but Rover became a deep water Baptist (I had dammed up the stream). Modestine and I were small children then and life seemed so simple, but we lived it out in the seriousness of our parents and older siblings. Rover was not allowed in the house, but in time he became our protector on the outside both day and night. Daddy, like in the words of his song, even thought highly of him.

Well, it must have been a Monday. Mother was washing in her three tub setting out back of the house. Rover slept near her feet. The top of the hill going toward the church was visible to the left of us and the curve at the bottom of the hill was just off to the right of that same view. It was a lovely white house, airplane style, Mother called it, with a backdrop grove of plum, peach and pear trees. Out front the ever-present Highway 87. An hour could pass without so much as an automobile passing, still it was considered dangerous. We had been told sternly not to play near the road and surely not to attempt to cross it without permission. A truck loaded with logs from the vast Thicket could not stop without problems after topping the hill and heading South toward the town of Newton. So, it was the practice of drivers to blow their horns, shift into low gear and proceed slowly down the hill. There had been lots of accidents heading into the curve at the base of the hill. That morning it was different and I shall never forget it.

While Mother washed, Rover slept near her tubs. Daddy was away at work in the vast Thicket. The older children were at school that morning and I had not noticed that Modestine had wandered after her pet calf. Somehow the gate had been left open and Butter Ball had wandered out onto the road. Modestine merely wandered to her. About the same time a truck loaded with logs peaked the hill and the driver blew his horn before the descent. He must have seen Modestine and Butter Ball as we could hear him shifting the mighty truck into low gears and begin blowing hard on the horn. He blew again and then kept on blowing as he began his descent.

It was the long blowing of the horn that got my Mother's attention. She looked to her left and saw the log truck moving slowly down the hill. The man laid on the horn harder. When Mother looked to her right she saw her baby, Modestine, right there in the middle of Highway 87, right next to her precious Butter Ball. Both of them perched in front of the mailbox with head trained on the approaching truck, but standing still as stones! Mother screamed! Now, old Rover stood up and seemed to assess the situation.

Mother screamed, "Somebody, get that child!" as she started running toward Modestine. Old Rover started running, too! He clipped across the yard as if to answer Mother's cry. I thought, "There goes the dumbest dog in Texas. He's going to get himself killed, just like Modestine!" Pondering that unthinkable thought, praying for a miracle, I was frozen in place. I knew that Mother could not reach Modestine. Old Rover clipped away at the distance and I thought that he would attack the log truck. Instead, Rover ran full speed into little Modestine's head, knocking her from the truck's path. At that same moment, however, the truck's left front wheel ran over the center of Rover's body.

The driver managed to stop his truck near the Yellow Bayou and came running back up the road. He cried out his apology, thinking that he had hit the child. But, it was not so. He had run over a tall, bony, light-gray coated stray dog—Old Rover.

Amidst the commotion Butter Ball had wandered, free of danger, back across the road. Old Rover, my old Rover lay crushed at the side of the road. I raked my dog's body near me on the road where the impact had thrown him. In his closing moments, whenever his eyes would catch mine, he would waggle his tail. Old Rover, my Rover did that until he died.

When I get to Heaven, if Old Rover ain't there, I'm going to organize a protest and march on the great white throne! Greater love hath no human being than what Rover showed that day. He laid down his life for a friend.

It was only a love song when Daddy sang it in Mississippi, in the Thicket's railroad years. John Lomax and his wife, Ruby T. Lomax, recorded him singing it in 1940 in our living room. It is on one of the fifty-two recordings of Henry Truvillion in the Library of the U.S.

Congress, all recorded by John Lomax from 1920-1940, in a project to preserve original American folklore. It is listed by its first verse line "'Possum was an Evil Thing," but its correct title is "Ol' Rover." Sometimes men worked while Daddy sang it. On other occasions, it was just for entertainment. But, with years to ponder that Monday morning, it has taken on new meaning. As it appears here I have added a few verses to the tune to accentuate the memory.

(Chorus)   Old Rover, oh, hoo-hoo!
               Old Rover, oh, hoo-hoo!
               That's me a'talking—Boy,
               Oh hoo, hoo—hoo—hoo.

        Danger was a lurking then—
        A horn—long blowing stark!
        A mother screaming for her child—
        And then old Rover barked.

(Chorus)

        Treasured is the Thicket's lore—
        Of people strong of heart,
        Of children and their freedom dreams—
        There where old Rover barked.

(Chorus)

        Memory is a sacred gift—
        Of how our lives were marked,
        And love will ever kiss the wind
        Into which Rover barked.

(Chorus)

JAMES THOMAS JACKSON

Waiting in Line at the Drugstore

I am black. I am a writer and I want to place full credit where it belongs for the direction my life has taken: on a photography studio and a drugstore on Main Street in Houston, Texas.

When I was thirteen, I dropped out of school, bought a bike for $13 (secondhand and innately durable) and went to work as a messenger for the Owl Foto Studio. Each day we processed film which I picked up as raw rolls on my three routes. That was great: a bike and job are supreme joys to a thirteen-year-old.

The Owl Studio, on a nondescript street named Brazos (very Texan), was located in a white stucco building that blended unobtrusively into the rest of the neighborhood, which was mostly residential. The area was predominantly white, and though it did not smack of affluence, it was not altogether poverty stricken either. Six blocks away was the drugstore, where I had to go first thing each morning for coffee, cakes, doughnuts, jelly rolls, milk, cigarettes, whatever—anything the folks at the Owl wanted. My trip amounted to picking up "breakfast" for a crew of six: three printer-developers, one wash-dry man, the roll-film man and the foreman. The drugstore was the biggest challenge of my young life. Being thirteen is doubtless bad enough for white male youths, but for blacks—me in particular—it was pure dee hell. Going to this drugstore each morning was part of my job; it was required of me. With my dropping out of school and all, my parents would have whipped my behind till it roped like okra if I had tried to supply them with reasons for not wanting to go. So, I gritted my teeth and, buoyed by the power of my Western Flyer, rode on down there.

The place had your typical drugstore look: sundries, greeting cards, cosmetics, women's "things," pharmaceuticals—but most instantly fetching was the large, U-shaped lunch counter. White-uniformed waitresses dispensed eats and sweet drinks of varying kinds: from cakes, donuts and pies to cups of the freshest smelling, strongest tasting coffee one could ask for. In the morning, there were countless servings of ham, bacon, sausages and eggs and mounds of hash-brown potatoes. At lunch there was a "Blue Plate Special"—three vegetables and a meat dish. Oh, they were together, no doubt about that.

My beef was that I was forbidden to sit at that counter. If any black wanted service whether for himself or, like me, for those he worked for—he simply had to stand and wait until all the white folks were served. Those blacks who went contrary to this were worked over something fierce, often by those mild-mannered Milquetoasts who looked as if they wouldn't hurt a fly. A fly, no; but an uppity nigger, in a minute.

I had once witnessed the beating of a black brother at the drugstore and heard tales of other beatings elsewhere. Clean and sanitary as the drugstore was, I preferred the ghetto (though we didn't call it that then). There, at least, we had the freedom to roam all over our stretch of black territory and could shuck our feelings of enforced inferiority as soon as we were on common ground.

Yet I went to the drugstore each morning with my order of coffee, cakes and whatever, written out and clutched firmly in my hand. And each time I was confronted with rows of white folks, seated at the counter and clamoring for attention. I did what I was expected to do: I waited, all the while hating it.

Especially that kind of waiting. As those white faces stared at my black face, I stood conspicuously in a spot near the counter, wanting not to be there, to be somewhere else.

My film pickups were not like this at all. I simply went in a store, picked up a small sack of roll film and split. After all, we provided twenty-four-hour service, and every son-of-a-buck and his brother wanted to see how his pictures came out. It was only the drugstore bit that bugged me.

While waiting near the counter one morning, I realized that I was leaning on a bookcase. I had seen it before but had ignored it because I was in a hurry to get served and get the hell out of there. The case was about four feet high and held perhaps six rows of hardcover books. The sign said "Lending Library." I began looking idly at the books, studying the titles and names of authors, so many unfamiliar to me. But the jackets were impressive, alluring, eye-catching.

One book caught my fancy: *Out of the Night,* the bestseller by Jan Valtin. I opened it, glanced at the fly pages and came across a poem by William Ernest Henley:

> Out of the night that covers me
> Black as the pit from pole to pole
> I thank whatever gods may be
> For my unconquerable soul.

Then I turned to the beginning of Valtin's narrative, read that first page, and then the second. Eleven pages later, going on twelve, hoping to get to thirteen, I heard the white waitress call my name. My order was ready. I folded a corner of the page and tried to hide the book so no one would take it before I could get back the next day.

I picked up the food and wheeled back to the studio—slowly. My mind was a fog—I had never begun a real book before. All the way back, I felt different from before. Something was happening to me, and I didn't quite know what to make of it. Somehow I didn't feel the "badness" that I usually felt when I returned from the drugstore.

The next day, my usual waiting was not the same. I went from page thirteen to page twenty-seven . . . twenty-eight, pinned a corner down, returned to the studio, delivered my routes, went home, thought and wondered. God, I wondered, when would tomorrow come? The promise of tomorrow, of course, was the difference.

Many mornings later I finished reading Valtin's book. But there was another that looked interesting: *The Grapes of Wrath* by John Steinbeck. (We weren't as poor, I discovered, as those people.) Then *Tobacco Road* by Erskine Caldwell.

A year passed, and I discovered a black library branch at Booker T. Washington High. An elderly friend of mine in the ghetto who had noticed the change in me made a list of things to ask for: Countee Cullen's poem "Heritage," Charles W. Chestnutt's "The Wife of His Youth," Walter White's "Fire in the Flint"; also Frederick Douglass, Paul Lawrence Dunbar, Jean Toomer—how was I to read them all?

Find a way, my friend said.

All the while I kept going to the drugstore each morning. I must have read every worthwhile book on that "Lending Library" shelf. But during this period, something strange happened: my waiting time got shorter and shorter each morning. I could hardly get five pages read before my order was handed to me with—of all things a sense of graciousness from the waitresses. I didn't understand it.

Later on I went off to World War II. My mind and attitudes were primed for the books yet to come and for the words that were to come out of me. I was eighteen then and a drop-out, but I was deep into the wonderful world of literature and life. I found myself, and my niche, in the word. Who would have thought that a drugstore could provide such a vista for anyone? And my waits at the counter? I keep wondering: which way would I have gone had I not waited?

Good question.

BOB LEE

A Hunt in the Big Thicket

Dewitt Adams was no political thinker, but a man of rural genius surpassing any I know or will ever know. He was a gentle giant, full of affection and a vast knowledge. He stood six foot four inches and weighed two hundred and fifty pounds. His skin was the darkest ebony and his eyes, a steely brown. He was strong on moral qualities and possessed the look of a biblical character in logging overalls.

Dewitt's gifted intellect had been tutored by the great forest of East Texas. It was his refuge and he lived out his days there. They were days filled with praising the ideals of the family bond. "The Big Thicket," he would say, "is like a mother. She cares for you while you live, supplies you with the resources of food and, when you die, brings you back to her forest to lay you to rest."

When Dewitt was born in the Big Thicket, delivered by a midwife in August 1900, it is said that lightning struck across the sky, and for the remainder of the night, all that was heard was the wise old owl repeating, WHO? WHO? WHO?

At 4 A.M. one East Texas morning, Uncle Dewitt and I were having breakfast. It was the morning of a big squirrel hunt that we had planned for weeks. I was living with Uncle Dewitt and Aunt Cricket while I was working on a story about law and order in Newton County. My lovely, graceful Aunt Cricket was refilling Uncle Dewitt's cup with Colombian coffee that a friend had sent them from Chicago. I was sitting there, talking and carrying on about the horrible things the Republican administration had done and was doing to the American masses, making many of them homeless due to a lack of jobs. Uncle looked at me over the rim of his glasses and said, "This world has changed many times and I still live as I always have."

I reminded him that it was President Rutherford B. Hayes of the Republican party in the late 1800s who disenfranchised Southern blacks.

He had pulled federal support from Southern states, a move that established segregation laws. Uncle Dewitt never said a word. For all the years we had spent together I had never heard him say one negative word about any human or animal. To him, gossiping and slandering were sinful. But, on this morning the subject of politics somehow turned to racial hatred.

I was talking about the Ku Klux Klan and today's skinheads. He chuckled at the mention of skinheads. He had a laugh like Santa Claus. "Between you and me," he looked at me with dark eyes, "this cup of coffee is like a racist—ain't worth a sour pear tree. And as for them 'Republicans,' Me an' Cricket both are Republicans." I dropped my fork into my plate of eggs and grits then turned to Aunt Cricket. "Yes, honey," she replied sweetly. Why? I questioned. Why? Uncle Dewitt answered simply and firmly, "Because it was Lincoln—a Republican— who freed the slaves." That ended our discussion of politics forever.

That morning as we entered the hunting zone, from way atop a pine tree, an old, wise owl asked, "Who? Who? Who?" Uncle Dewitt looked up and said, "It's me: Dewitt Adams—son of Doc and Dollie Adams." He smiled over at me and said, "We can go now."

As we hunted, the sun's luminous rays alternated with black shadows among the tall East Texas pines. Uncle Dewitt had taught me early on how to hunt squirrel and we had enough to make a fine supper. Get only what is needed, he would say.

While hunting we talked of the night's supper with collard or turnip greens, sweet potatoes, prepared in honey and butter with rice and fried okra. Of course, there would be black-eyed peas and hot water corn bread. Aunt Cricket would cook the squirrel meat slowly in garlic, butter and onions. She was probably already heating up the wood stove, listening for the sound of our shotguns to signal our return from the hunt. Until then, she'd be squeezing the lemons for lemonade or preparing the ice tea.

After a while, we came to a log near the creek and sat down to enjoy the surroundings. In the creek, the sun perch were feeding, and all around us were the sounds of squirrels playing in the trees. They seemed to be laughing that they weren't the night's meal and that the hunt had ended. We could also hear the fast knocking of a woodpecker, shopping for his meal. Uncle Dewitt stared into the creek. He had lived in this forest for eighty-four years and it made me wonder just what was on his mind. He took his gourd from his shoulder and drank, then passed it to me. I had seen him with this gourd for years, but never thought to ask where he had gotten it. Now, I held it and observed the fine craftsmanship in both the elongated gourd and the leather strap. The strap was fitted with seven beads, most likely Indian or African in creation. The gourd had a deep varnished look, accented by the beaded strap at both ends, and a leather stopper or cap. The gourd played a very important part in rural life. It was used as a dipper; for storing milk or seeds; and even as an eating bowl. They came in many shapes and sizes and had a lot of uses. "Great spirits came for the durable plant of the gourd," Uncle Dewitt chimed in. I drank from the gourd and enjoyed the cool water.

Just then, a wild sound broke the silence of the forest and something in the sky brought Uncle Dewitt to his feet. It was a thin, clear, flutelike sound that repeated steadily. Uncle Dewitt stared skyward and listened as if it might be Gabriel blowing his horn. Instead, it was the calling of wild geese flying overhead. By the time I finally saw them they were just a V-shaped speck against the Texas sky. Still, they were a mysterious and wonderful sight. "These geese have been coming this way for thousands of years," Uncle Dewitt offered. He was just as excited now as I imagined he had been as a child. The geese seemed to fascinate him. I wonder what guides them across the mountains, I said aloud. Uncle Dewitt looked at me, "God guides them."

Soon, the geese passed out of sight. Their sweet sound grew faint and distant and then, they were gone. I thought to myself, that despite some men's conceit, the eagle, hawk and geese remain the most magnificient flying machines. Looking over to Uncle Dewitt, he seemed frozen.

"Paw, Paw," I whispered, "let's go." He turned to me with his ancient, ebony face and whispered back, "Go where, Junior?" We sat back down on the log and listened to the morning of the forest.

I never suspected this would be the last time that I would be with this old man of the Big Thicket whom I loved and admired so greatly. I never knew it would be our last hunt.

History books will not record Uncle Dewitt's life, but he was history, and he was my personal hero in my own family. Since his death, I have not hunted in the Thicket and even gave away my shot gun to an old friend. In the Fall I return to the Big Thicket to hear the sounds of the forest; to listen to the squirrels; and to listen for that great sound moving through the sky. I return also to think of all the good folks resting there, like my hero: Uncle Dewitt.

PEARL GARRETT CRAYTON

My Hellion Parrain[1]

I started out in this world with a mama and a daddy that I thought I could hold onto until either they died or I did. When I was real young I didn't know nothing about losing somebody that I could still see and touch and talk to. Even then I knowed that family folks had falling outs and didn't want to talk to or be around one another for long spells. And I knowed that some folks moved away from home, went to far-off places and didn't come back to see their families but every once in a while. Losses like that I could understand. But, the worst kind of way to lose a mama and a daddy is worse than all the other ways put together; even worse than death.

I don't know how come I had to be the one to find this out.

Ain't nobody nowhere had no better mama and daddy than mine. Lord knows I'd give up the rest of my life to be able to go back behind this day to that sweet time before my mind got all messed up with knowing.

Though I don't hate him for it, it was all my Parrain's fault.

Folks out on Little River Lane Plantation, where I growed up, claimed he was a hellion; the worst that ever lived. Anytime he got drunk and started raising hell, it didn't do no good to call the sheriff. Wouldn't nobody never come.

One night the High Sheriff, Bill White, had a run-in with Parrain out at the house of the one-eyed Cajun who lived on the hill. Comed back with his eyes all blood-shot and his pistol missing. But didn't nobody make no fuss about it because everybody knowed the Cajun made his living making and selling moonshine. Most likely the High Sheriff didn't want nobody going around asking what was he doing out there in the middle of the night in the first place.

Parrain had the missing pistol and the shaming answer. So old Bill White let him raise all the hell he wanted to.

That's the tale I heard when I was growing up, but I didn't never know my Parrain to raise no hell. The worst I ever seed him do was sock Plug Aguillard in his old cat-gray eye for saying a cuss word in front of my Nen-Nen. No more than any other man woulda done to defend the honor of his wife. Old Plug knowed better anyhow. But he was three sheets in the wind at the time. My Parrain's fist sobered him up real quick.

Most tales that folks used to tell about my Parrain I didn't never believe. Like they said he was bad about running behind womens. The way I seed it, a man all laid back like him didn't never run behind nothing. He took his own good time about everything he did. Especially talking. He chewed on every word, then swallowed it and let it come rolling up from his belly, deep and rich. Words worth waiting for. And he walked as slow and easy as a cat stalking a bird, rippling his big, hard muscles with every move.

But he wasn't lazy slow and he wasn't weak easy. Everything about him looked strong and dangerous—his tall, stout body, his blacker than the heart of the Devil black skin; even his voice could rumble like thunder when his dander was up.

I knowed he didn't run behind womens because he was a good husband to Nen-Nen. So I figured them that accused him woulda done what they accused him of doing, if they'd been as good-looking as him.

Wouldn't none of my friends never go with me to my Parrain's house. My cousin Rena told me that something real bad was gonna happen to me there one day because my Parrain was such a awful bad hellion. "He got a John the Conqueror root." She warned me, "That's how he whipped the High Sheriff and got away with it. One of these days he gonna pull that thing out on you and paralyze you and ruin you for the rest of your life."

I didn't pay what she said no mind. What he did pull out on me wasn't a John the Conqueror root, but it ruined me in a way that I ain't never been able to tell. Still, I don't hate him for it.

I never knowed what I was stepping out into. It happened as slow and easy as my Parrain used to move.

Wasn't nothing wrong with me spending nights with my Parrain and Nen-Nen. Everybody did that. Out on the plantation every baby had to be christened into the church, so in case it died before it got old enough to stand for its own sins, it wouldn't wind up in Hell. Better than that, a Parrain and Nen-Nen stood to take a godchild in and raise it if the real mama and daddy died. Parrain, Nen-Nen and godchild had to live close, so we did.

At the time I didn't have sense enough to see it, but Parrain was planting seeds in my head for what happened later. Like he was getting me ready for the knowing that made me lose my mama and daddy.

He put it in my head that I was beautiful, not just good looking or cute, like black folks was supposed to be, but beautiful, like Shirley Temple. Me and him and Nen-Nen used to get in their old Model-T and drive all the way up to Templeville to buy me the prettiest dress in town. On account of my Parrain said homemade dresses ain't good enough for his godchild.

Them times I spent nights with them, especially on a Sunday, Parrain made a such a big fuss about putting flowers in my hair that we'd be late for church. Just any old flower wouldn't do. He'd send me out, then Nen-Nen; Parrain would look the flowers over and say something like, "Ain't I done told you ever since the day we christened this here child? The Lord didn't see fit to give me and you no children of our own. Me and you stood before God in his own house and got this here child. Ain't nothing but the best good enough for God and we gonna give it to him through this here child. Nothing but the best."

Nen-Nen, she'd be on pins and needles for him to hurry up and come on so we could start out for church. But she never did say nothing. Most times when they brought me along, we'd show up early enough to hear the pastor's sermon. Which was early enough for me.

But that's only one of the reasons we never did get to church on Sundays until the best possible time. On account of Parrain never was laid back on no other day as far as he was laid back on Sunday mornings. Getting ready to go to church, he didn't move hardly fast enough for the eye to see. Except for one time. When Nen-Nen got up from the breakfast table one Sunday morning and fell flat on the floor, he moved. Before that I didn't know that a human being could move so fast or be so strong. Nen-nen was a heavy-set woman, but Parrain picked her up like she wasn't nothing but a baby doll. Look to me like the same second that he picked her up, we was in that Model-T on our way to the doctor's in Morgan.

But didn't nothing do no good.

A few days after Nen-Nen's funeral, I stopped by Parrain's house on my way home from school. He was setting in his rocking chair in front of the fireplace with a paper in his hand like he knowed I was gonna stop by.

He handed the paper to me and told me to read it to him. I couldn't hardly believe my own eyes.

"Parrain, is you fixing to die?" I asked.

"No, but I can't wait 'til the last minute to get ready," he told me. "Didn't you see how they didn't do right by your Nen-Nen in her obituary? They ain't told half the good she done. So I aim to write my own obituary and get it right before I go."

I looked at the sheet of paper in my hand with not enough writing on it to fill up more than half a page.

"Ain't you got more than this to say about what you done done?" I asked my Parrain.

That hit him like dirty dishwater flung in his face. He downed his eyes, something my Parrain didn't hardly never do. Then, quick like a rubber band stretched out too far that got let loose, he went smaller right before my eyes.

And I got to wondering how come what I said shamed him so.

"I'm working on it," he said after a while. "I just got started. I got lots more to write. But I want you to promise me you'll read it over me when my time come."

That was the first time I ever seed Death on anybody. Wasn't nothing on his face, nothing in the sound of his voice, nothing nowhere around him that changed. But in the silence, between touching a thing and feeling yourself touch it, in one part of one second split into a million parts, I seed Death on Parrain.

Ain't nothing in the world I'd ever seed before made me feel sadder than that sight.

Next time I laid eyes on my Parrain he was setting on the front bench at our church. Now that knocked me offa my foots. We was amongst the first folks to get to the church house on Sundays for Sunday School. And church never did start until after that was over. So how come Parrain comed so early?

Soon as Parrain seed us walk in he got up and told Daddy he wanted to get baptized.

That was the week after Thanksgiving.

"Before you get baptized you gotta first be a mourner," Daddy told him. "Then you got to pray to get religion."

In them days sinners had to pray and trouble the Lord about their sins for about a week or two. They had to tell about their travels with the Lord in twelve o'clock prayer meetings every day. Then they had to come through with religion and shout and carry on about how thcy done got converted and saved from a life of sin and a burning Hell.

"I ain't seed no chariot of fire, and I ain't talked to no angels, and I ain't gonna lie about it," Parrain told Daddy, "but look at me, blacker than the black side of the moon. So you know for yourself I done been 'buked and I done been scorned. You tell me I gotta be a mourner. Shucks, I been mourning alla my life. And I done raised hell, and I done drunk moonshine, and I done worked my fingers to the bone. I done had plenty and I done lost plenty. Now here I is. I give myself to the Lord who made me to do with me what He please."

Parrain didn't just say this with words. He pulled hisself up tall, and he upped his chin just enough to look down at everthing else in the world. And look to me like he got blacker, burning black, flashing black lightning outta his eyes.

Daddy was a deacon and Sunday School teacher, so he had some say about what went on at the church. He sort of backed up into his ownself and told Parrain that he'd talk to the pastor about baptising him.

"Next Sunday!"

Parrain thundered the lowest thunder I ever did hear. Them two words just eased inside my ears and bust wide open. Not with sound, but with power. Them two words told me that ain't nobody better buck Parrain.

Standing before him, Daddy just about fainted.

Back in them days, the only place for folks to do their baptizings was in the rivers. Which is why they always baptized in spring or summer. But that day I'm talking about was in December, much too cold for to be wading into any river.

Looking at Daddy's face, I could see the memory of all the most awful tales about Parrain going through his mind. I could see Daddy's eyes looking for some sign that Parrain had his .38 Special on him, and I could have told him that my Parrain never did go nowhere without his pistol. I saw Daddy trying to swallow his heart. He scratched in his hair like he was trying to dig up some words to put Parrain's mind at ease. Then he said, "Well, I ain't never knowed the church to turn down nobody wanting to get baptized."

In church services later when Daddy brought up the matter, didn't nobody speak one word against it.

During the week Mama sewed up a white baptizing gown for Parrain. And come the next Sunday, our pastor and two deacons waded out into the river, dressed in overcoats, and baptized him.

The next Sunday after the baptizing, Parrain made hisself a Sunday School teacher. The pastor already had the grown folks class and Daddy taught the children. Parrain told them he wanted to teach the big children. So they divided us up at eleven.

Parrain didn't never teach not one class.

"I got a dollar for the first person who can say the 23rd Psalm by heart." That's the first thing he told us. Then he opened his Bible and read the 23rd, one time. Right off my cousin, Sam, jumped up and tried to go for that dollar. When he fell flat on his face, Slow Kidd tried.

The good thing was that when they made the first mistake, Parrain read that verse right. So just setting there listening to them that tried, the rest of us learned enough to go for it too. We spent the whole Sunday School hour tryin', but didn't nobody get the dollar that day.

"Next Sunday the dollar goes to the one who can say the longest Psalm by heart," Parrain told us. "So be sure you count the verses of whichever one you study." That's the way he dismissed class.

In them days they was paying four bits a hundred for picking cotton and six bits a day for hoeing from kin-to-can't. So didn't nobody need to tell us to open up them Bibles that week.

I got the 18th Psalm down pat backwards and forward. By the

next Sunday morning I could say it in my sleep without stumbling. But, it didn't do me no good.

Slow Kidd wasn't never wrapped too tight. When Parrain said "longest," he meant a Psalm longer than the one that everybody else could say by heart. But Slow Kidd, he went and took him at his word and went and got the 119 Psalm down pat! He even got alla them little words at the tops like "Pe," "Mem," "Ain" and alla that down pat. Couldn't tell for the life of him what none of it meant. But he said it all by heart. Didn't miss one word.

"Next Sunday our champ, Mr. Slow Kidd, will go for the dollar after everybody else done failed," Parrain told us. "I know that a man with a good head on him like he got gonna win alla my money if I don't give the rest of y'all a chance. And I know he don't mind being last because he gonna win plenty more times."

Not if the rest of us could help it.

Didn't take long for the grown folks to notice that children all over Little River Lane Plantation and the Rockford Place was studying their Bibles night and day. Them same folks what done told alla them hateful tales about my Parrain started going around talking about what a good Sunday School teacher he was.

Next time Parrain asked me to read his obituary, he had put in there about his baptizing and Sunday School teaching. Three whole lines.

"That's better," I told him after I read it.

"But it ain't good enough," he said in a sad voice.

Wasn't long before Parrain joined the usher board and Benevolent Society. Society members had to set up with the sick; work their crops and gardens; wash and iron their clothes and do everything else that needed to be done until the sick got back on their foots.

Parrain out-did everybody doing good works. The folks got to talking about what a miracle the Lord done worked on "that old hellion." Folks was about ready to crown him a saint when one monthly meeting day Shep Junior did some cussing on the church house grounds. Parrain whopped Shep so hard that the man turned a sommersault before he fell to the ground. Quick like lightning he grabbed him, pulled him back up on his foots and whopped him again. It took four mens to hold Parrain off the poor fellow long enough for him to run off. He even forgot his riding horse. Maybe he figured he could get away faster on foots. He just about out-runned his own shadow.

A little over a year and few months after Parrain got baptized, when Spring rolled around again, I went to his house one Saturday morning because it was one of them warm Louisiana mornings, too pretty for anybody to be in the house all by hisself. Blue and lavender morning glory and cypress vines with itsy-bitsy blood-red blossoms had covered the fences on both sides all along Little River Lane on the way to Rockford Place. Honeysuckle vines had wrapped theirselves around just enough stumps and fallen logs to sweten the air with their cream and butter blossoms. The grass along the sides of the lane was sprinkled with yellow, blue, pink, red, white and lavender flowers. There was big patches of blooming clover with pink and white buttercups swaying and bowing in the cool breeze. Wisteria and mimosa trees, fruit trees and dogwoods was all waving pretty blossoms at the sky, calling all the angels down to see the prettiest sights on earth.

In some spots birds was singing. But in other spots the quiet was so deep that I could almost feel it with my hands. That quiet stopped me and held me to listen a while. All along the lane these little patches, where look like no sound had never touched, showed me, right there in the midst of the sweet singing and the slowing colors and all the yummy, yummy good smells, little scraps of death.

I found Parrain setting in his rocking chair on his front porch. Funniest thing was, when he seed me, he didn't even look my way. And I don't remember hearing him speak neither. All I remember is that he had this big tin box laying on his lap. First thing he did was hand it to me.

"Open it," a voice said. Not Parrain's voice. Out of the breeze or out of the floor or somewhere the sound came.

Inside I saw a big .45 pistol like sheriff use and a little bank book.

"Your name and my name on that bank book," the voice that I didn't recognize told me. "It's yours now. From now on."

For some reason I knowed that the second I touched that little book, something awful was gonna happen, something that I would never, never be able to straighten out, not for the rest of my life. For some reason I knowed that this gift of money was much, much more than all the pretty flowers he picked for my hair.

I had been raised to say "Thank you" for all good things that comed to me. But that day I couldn't force the words outta my mouth.

Then, he handed me his obituary. Two full pages.

Halfway through reading it to him, I knowed he'd put alla his heart into it this time. He hadn't writ hisself just borned into the world. He writ his mama and daddy was blessed with him. He writ hisself "touched by the Holy Ghost and turned from sinful ways and washed in the blood of the Lamb of God." He writ hisself doing for the Lord's little ones as He hisself said folks oughta do. He writ hisself a good and loving husband, a good neighbor, the kind of man that any other man would be proud to be.

"Parrain, you done it!" I told him when I finished reading. "Ain't nobody nowhere never had no obiturary this good."

He settled hisself back into his rocking chair so far that the wood of the chair and the flesh of his face became the same. Although he didn't smile, I could see that he was satisfied.

Then I thought out loud, "You been knocking yourself out well over a year now working on stuff to put in your obiturary. I sure do hope some folks remember some of what you done writ."

"It ain't for my obiturary I been scuffling so hard," the voice of the rocking chair face told me. "I did it all so my child would be proud of me."

"I ain't never knowed you to have no child," I told him.

I saw him settle hisself further back into the rocking chair. Then, one of them patches of quiet I passed on the lane on my way to see him comed up. It fell all over that porch so hard until I could hear how it was before God made the world—when there hadn't never been nothing around to make no sound. Never before and never since did so much quiet hit my ears.

After while I heard a voice from far away coming from deep, deep down into the wood of the rocking chair.

"Way long back when I was in my wild ways, I had me a outside woman."

I remembered the times I'd heard folks say the same thing about him. Just the same, hearing him say it hurt me. On account of only the worst kind of mens did things like that. Dirty, low-down mens who had outside womens didn't do nothing but bring trouble and bad diseases into their homes and made their families suffer.

"My woman, she had a child by me. But she had a husband. He knowed my child wasn't his. But he raised it like it was his. Hurtingest thing ever troubled my soul was seeing my own child, my only child, growing up calling some other man 'daddy.' But wasn't no other way to keep respect. Once you lose your child's respect, you lost your child."

As far as I knowed back then, outside womens didn't have no husbands. They was loose in the world, not decent enough for no man to marry. And they all lived in town because overseers wouldn't never let no loose woman live on no plantation. They didn't do nothing but cause trouble and spread bad diseases. I wondered where in the world did my Parrain find a loose woman with a husband?

"Where your child at now, Parrain?" I asked.

Only the quiet patch from back along the lane answered my question.

I got to thinking about the birthday Parrain writ on his obituary that I been reading well over a year. Already I'd figured out that he was past sixty. What I did was take forty from that. I knowed he couldn't been no older than that when his child was born. That left enough years for the bastard to be grown and gone by now. I sure didn't want whoever it was showing up and ruining the little reputation Parrain done scuffled so hard to build up.

"Is your child a boy or girl?" I asked. Then I seed he done nodded off, his head drooped to one side the way old folks do cat napping. Maybe he sleepy because he done set up all night getting his obituary straight, I told myself. So I sot down on the edge of the porch in front of him to wait 'til he woke up.

Too much time passed and too many questions got to troubling my mind. Like, how come I ain't never seed Parrain's child come to see him at his house, not even after Nen-Nen died? Ain't no other children never comed there, but me. And if he cared so much about his child that he knocked hisself out trying to make whoever it was proud of him, how come he ain't put that bastard's name on the bank book?

How come he put mine on there?

Finally, I got up and stood on the porch close to him and asked, "Parrain, your child ain't living nowhere close around here, is it?"

That's the first time I noticed how still he was. Things that ain't never had no life to move them don't never be as still as living things be right after they lose life. Before I touched him to make sure, before my hand got all the way down to his arm, the cold met me, stung me. Ain't no other cold like death.

I hollered and hollered and hollered.

Pretty soon, the folks who lived up the lane comed running. First thing they wanted to know was how it happened.

I knowed I couldn't never tell nobody all of it, so I didn't tell none of it. To this very day some folks claim I almost grieved myself to death over Parrain. But it wasn't grief that troubled my mind. It was questions. And too many memories of too many things that had happened over too many years of my life, too many tales I'd heard, too much was on my mind.

Most of the time I was just as sure as the sun is of shining that I wasn't the one. On account of I knowed my mama was too decent a woman to do what she would have to done done for me to be the one. But then, didn't I get all the money? How come? So one day I got up enough guts to ask Mama.

She denied it.

For the life of me, I tried to be a good child after that. If only I coulda got rid of alla them looking glasses that kept on showing me Parrain's face in mine.

It wasn't right for none of them to do me the way they did. Just to "keep respect" is the way Parrain put it with his final breath. But they didn't lose me; I lost them. On account of I don't know who's who no more. I wish they'd come clean with me and set me free of this devilish wondering. I'd think better of them if they did. If only they loved me enough to trust me to understand.

[1]Creole word for godfather.

JESSE GARFIELD TRUVILLION

A Child's Life in the Big Thicket:
A Love of Blackberries

It is a place in the heart for all seasons. Kind deeds were never lost there for in the vastness of that unique Southeast Texas forest every human being was going to need help sometime. In Newton and Jasper counties one seldom heard a negative word or a song too sad to lift your spirits. I am a child of that tall and dense forest, born in the first house finished for an African American in Wiergate, home of the great saw mills of the Southwest. It was a home along Highway 87 in one of the emancipation communities that was formed and that flourished in the midst of what was once more than three and a half million acres of land—The Big Thicket.

It is a sacred place formed of some great upheaval in Mother Nature's long story; a meeting place of the Southwestern deserts; the Central Plains; the Eastern forest; the Appalachian Mountains and the Southeastern swamps. The giant meteorite that formed what we call the Gulf of Mexico by its magnificent impact must have dammed into the Thicket its natural richness. The Thicket is a biological crossroads of North America. Scientists from the world community are students of the biological diversity, the ecosystems and the unique environment of that grand American Ark that I know of as "home."

My father, born in Brookhaven, Mississippi, came to the Thicket with the railroads and as a foreman for the Wier Long Leaf Lumber Company. My mother was born in Magnolia Springs, deep in the heart of the Thicket, a rose always in full bloom. Married in 1927, my parents were their children's favorite love story. Daddy called mother "Sweet" and she called him, "Honey." Seeing them kiss was a childhood delight, for they were setting the pattern for our own adult lives. They showed us "the ought to" of parenting. It was Daddy's testimony that Mother tasted like blackberries should—but better! "Blackberries," he said, were limited to a season but Mother's sweetness transcended such a situation. Of my parent's love five children were born, I am fourth and the last was Modestine. In our house Modestine was called Precious Sweetness, I think because she looked so much like Mother.

Taste gave definition to character in our Emancipation Community. The darker the berry the sweeter the taste permeated the ethics and ethnicity of my childhood years. Character had a certain taste to it and often was heard the proverb of good parenting, "Don't leave a bad taste in any situation." But, for a child the line between symbol and substance did not always clearly exist.

I love the sweetness of the Thicket's blackberries and keep that taste with me to this very day. It is a taste of appreciation: an unspoiled land, freely flowing clean waters, air born fresh and clean to every living thing and a heap of sunlight and shadow into which many forms of life freely roamed. Those berries spoke these qualities with every ounce of their juices and every inch of their tender skins.

Throughout my childhood, filled with a love of berries, the Thicket also held its share of danger and mystery within that dark forest. There was a time when the region was known for lawlessness. Lawlessness has always marked the path of human pioneering and the Thicket's people were no different. When into those woods the humans came, hatred came also—the race kind. It was Texas where American slavery lasted the longest and Southeast Texas, where hiding from and misusing the law was possible. The Thicket was the lair of murderers, thieves, gamblers and desperados. The U.S. Department of the Interior has long noted that the Thicket "gained a reputation for lawlessness" and that "The tenor of the Big Thicket lifestyles persists today in legend and lore, adding richness to the American Persona."

This "persona" meant danger to law abiders and especially law abiding African Americans. Racism haunted the Thicket much like the bigoted mindsets of the all-white Sumner, Florida, that led to the 1920s burning of the all-black Rosewood community. That racism led to the killing of adults, children, babies and even a dog. All of this was fresh memory for my dad on a day that had fate written in it for me. On that day, blackberries, those sweet rejoinders of the best that the Thicket had to give, were needed for a family dinner and I was given the honor of picking them.

Not long before that day I had been given a horse, named Old Bill, by my father. The whole family had turned out for the occasion as an old cattle truck ventured into our front yard and my Dad was called out. The driver led the horse out of the trailer and handed over the reigns to my dad, who in turn led the horse to me. It was a grand day when that horse arrived. Until then, we only had a mule, but then my dad handed me the rope and said, "Ride him, son, he's your horse." Time and sugar made me and Bill the best of friends. I had never ridden a horse, but eventually rode old Bill with no bridle or saddle, just the halter. We learned our way to each other on trips to pick berries. And so it was to be on that morning when I was sent to pick berries and return them before noon so that pies could be made for supper.

I ventured into the Piney Woods in a carefree spirit thinking the only danger out there was snakes. Berries grew where there were clearings in the forest, especially along the Yellow Bayou with its many pastures. In short order, I picked two buckets of blackberries with Old Bill near me to warn of approaching snakes. Horses won't stay near a snake, so I knew not to tread where Old Bill signaled fear. I collected the filled buckets on a tree limb, mounted my horse and headed, I thought, for home. Old Bill obeyed my word signals, moving through the heavy brush—there were no trails nearby—so we were guided by the sun toward home.

Bill and I walked for a long while and I wondered why we had not reached Highway 87. All I needed to do was find the highway and take it north, then cross the Yellow Bayou to home, but the woods were thick and dark and deep. Except for the occasional bird call there was silence—nothing reverberated through the depths of the woods from the highway—just silence.

In the Thicket a man was known by his holler, a loud call that sounded through the forest. My Dad had a holler that communicated directions, signaled a message or gave a distress cry. Developed over years on the railroad, I heard it in the fields, while driving cattle, when the hunt was over or when it was time to go home. The quietude of the woods gave distance to Dad's hollers.

Old Bill and I were walking on through the thick brush of the ever-unfamiliar woods. By the sun I knew that it was mid-afternoon, past the time given for my return. Suddenly, my father's holler broke through the silence, "My Son, Ho!!" I turned to Bill, "I didn't know he was coming out to pick berries, too. Let's stop here and let him catch up with us." We waited.

Then, Daddy's holler went up again through the silence, "My Son, Ho!!" I turned again to Bill, "I think Daddy is lost. Let's turn back and find him."

Very soon he hollered a third time, but with distress in his call, "My Son, Ho!!!!"

"Dad is hurt!" I said, "Let's trot, Bill. I may waste a few berries, but we need to hurry to help him!" Going toward the sound and coming to a clearing, we found him leaning on a post. He was crying like a child. Only in church had I witnessed him cry before. "Hand me your buckets and get down off your horse, son."

There was a barbed wire fence there and we let Old Bill jump over it to where Daddy was leaning. Dad cried as I crossed over into his arms. We sat there, on the ground, until he stopped crying.

"Do you remember crossing the Yellow Bayou, son?" he asked. "Did you not see the fence near the water?" I had entered the other Thicket where danger and lawlessness and racism were made manifest in the form of a white man who had sworn to shoot any black man seen on his property.

"For the last few hours you've been on that man's property, son."

Then, we started home with Old Bill walking behind us. "Look at the sun. Home is not that way, son. Home is back this way. You've been lost a long time."

I thought that he was lost only to discover that I was the lost one. I discovered more than that on that fateful day of berry picking. I had discovered the measure of a father. I was a boy, unknowingly lost in the Piney Woods. Even a white man would have thought twice about harming a little, black boy on a horse, with two buckets of blackberries. But, a full grown black man was a different matter! It was with a sure knowledge of the danger to himself that that man came into the woods looking for his son. He knew, by the amount of time that I had been gone that I had to be lost. There would be many other times, too, but on that spring day, Henry Truvillion, the railroad section boss and a man who knew the many seasons of being a man, showed me the stuff that a father is made of—he came for me, his son.

PHYLLIS W. ALLEN

The Red Swing

Two weeks ago I was a grown man with a life in the city. I had a wife, a mortgage and all the other responsibilities that signal manhood. Then I got a late night call saying that Aunt Meg was critically ill and asking for me. That phone call transformed me back into a scared little boy.

My wife and I made hurried preparations and after a high speed car trip we were at Aunt Meg's bedside.

Normally invincible Aunt Meg lay still and small in the hospital bed, her breathing barely perceptible. The hand I grasped in mine was cool, veined and frighteningly fragile. But, her grip was strong.

"I'm glad that you're here. I was waiting for you," she'd said in a whisper barely audible over the steady swish of the respirator.

"You know I could never refuse an invitation from you," trying for lighthearted when all I felt was fear. I was losing her and we both knew it.

Within the hour Aunt Meg was dead and I was back at her house, mine now, the place where I grew up. It was a place I hadn't visited frequently in recent years. But once inside it was as if I had never left. My childhood came back in a flood of familiar sights and smells. Standing there looking into the back yard, I could hear her voice.

"Boy, come in here and stop staring at them. Acting like you've never seen anybody play before," Aunt Meg would shout through the rough, weathered screen door.

I tried to pretend that I didn't know what she meant and answered, "I'm not staring at nobody, just standing here trying to catch a breeze. It's too hot in the house."

But she was right. I was standing on the cluttered front porch watching the four children, all about my age, playing on the thick green lawn that shimmered like an oasis in the August heat. I'd stand for hours on the screened porch, hiding behind dusty stacked boxes, overflowing ivy pots and yellowing newspapers that dated back before my birth watching those kids as they played.

I'd lived with Aunt Meg ever since Mama and Daddy were killed in a fire at the factory where they both worked.

The day of my parents' funeral, Aunt Meg told me that I was coming to live with her. I remember Mama and Daddy lying there still and much too quiet with a kind of waxy look, like the candles that we used during thunderstorms. "I am not very good with children. Really never been around them, but I'll do right by you," she'd said, tucking my small hand into her large rough one.

Mama and Daddy had always been different. That's why I never had friends, except for one, Andy Simons. That was because he was an outcast too. He never had a daddy and his mama got drunk. No one was allowed to bring him home either. I didn't know why I wasn't invited to birthday parties or to classmate's homes until Andy said, "Get wise. It's your folks. Look at 'em—you mama's White and your daddy's Black. Folks don't like that. Ain't you never noticed before?"

I thought about it then and realized that they *were* different. I guess I'd always known it, but it never seemed strange that Daddy's warm, strong hands were the color of the heavy mahogany furniture in our living room, while Mama's tiny, fat soft hands were the same shade as the inside of the honeymoon seashell on the shelf that I wasn't allowed to touch. I didn't think it was strange. They were just Mama and Daddy.

Other than Aunt Meg, my mama's aunt, no relatives ever visited us. Daddy's family was all dead. Mama had other family; they just didn't come to see us. There were grandparents, aunts, uncles and lots of cousins. I knew because I'd seen the pictures that Aunt Meg brought whenever she came to visit.

Mama once told me when I asked why we never saw them: "A long time ago I had to choose. I could have my family, who I loved. Or I could have your daddy. I could not have both. I chose your daddy."

But we had Aunt Meg and she visited often. Every time she came, she told Mama about the family. One time she said, "Maybe they will forgive you some day soon."

Mama said, in a voice I'd never heard her use before. "Meggie, I don't want anyone to forgive me for marrying the man I love and having a beautiful son. If they don't want to be a part of it, then that's their loss."

I think that's why I miss Mama so much, because she made everything so clear. We were a family. She loved me and she loved Daddy. That was it, pure and simple.

After I came to live with Aunt Meg, life wasn't so simple. There were rules, lots of rules. Most of them had to do with people who didn't like me because of Mama and Daddy.

That's how I learned the names of the kids next door. Aunt Meg's number one rule was, *don't go next door.* Don't look at, talk to or wave at Heather, April, Trey or Ben.

Not ever.

One day shortly after I came to Aunt Meg's house, I was sitting on the steps of the screened back porch. Heather and Ben were playing cowboys and seemed to be having a real good time. I inched closer and closer to the fence, drawn by the sound of laughter. At the same time I realized that it had stopped, I looked up into the prettiest and coldest set of blue eyes I'd ever seen.

I heard, "You're not supposed to be by our fence. You little half-breed nigger." Then she threw back her head, tossing blond curls in the wind and laughing at a joke I didn't understand.

She laughed until Ben said, "Aw, Heather, what's you want to bother him for? He's in his own yard. Daddy only said he couldn't come in ours."

"Yeah, but Daddy says we're not to be nice to him, because if you're nice to them they forget their place."

After that day, when Heather was around, I made sure that I stayed safely hidden on the porch. But sometimes when April came out by herself, we'd talk through the fence. She wasn't really Heather, Ben and Trey's sister. She was their cousin, an orphan like me. Her mom died. Her dad married a woman who didn't like children, so she came to live with her aunt and uncle.

April was different from Heather and her brothers. They were fair, with hair the color of straw and ice blue eyes. April was a creamy apricot color, with hair like sable silk. She had deep golden eyes that sometimes looked green. She liked to read, just like I did. We would talk about books we'd read or wanted to read, and we'd talk about what it was like not to have parents.

I really liked the fact that when I showed her the picture of my parents and me at the beach she didn't ask why my mama and my daddy were different colors. She said, "Your mama is pretty and your daddy looks so strong. I'll bet they really miss you." I knew I missed them, but I'd never thought about them missing me. April was like that. She made you think of things that you normally wouldn't.

We always had to be careful not to get caught visiting through the fence. My Aunt Meg and her Uncle Henry didn't like each other, and made it clear we shouldn't like each other either.

I heard Aunt Meg call April's uncle an ignorant, no-account bigot. She said, "I swear if that man could draw money based on his ignorance, he'd be rich."

When I asked Aunt Meg what a bigot was, she explained that was a person who hated another person for no reason at all. I wondered if that made me a bigot, because I hated Heather and her brothers for no reason that I could think of. Well, other than their not being very nice to April or me.

One weekend there was a big party next door to celebrate Heather's birthday. The following Monday two men came up in a truck and set up a big shiny red swing set. It was just like the one at the Wonderland Park. After that, I spent every day wedged down into my hiding place on the porch watching Heather, April, Trey and Ben play on the new swing. I wanted to swing too. I wanted one chance on the bright shiny red swing.

About two weeks later, I was sitting on the back porch. Aunt Meg had gone into town, and I'd persuaded her I was old enough to be left at home alone. Her last words were, "Now don't you go out of this yard. You hear me?"

"Yes Ma'am," I said without looking up from my porch hiding place.

After Aunt Meg left I sat on the porch, looking at the shiny red swing. Just then April came out the back door.

"Whatcha doing?" she called out.

"Nothing, just sitting," I answered, jumping down and heading for the fence. I knew there would be trouble if her uncle heard us talking.

"I'm here alone. Everybody else went to the Rotary Club picnic, but I couldn't go 'cause I'm being punished," she said. There wasn't a trace of suffering in her voice. "I'm not supposed to come outdoors, but I want to swing. You want to come over? There's no one to see you. I saw your Aunt Meg leaving."

"Naw, I'd better not. Aunt Meg would skin me alive if she caught me." But even as I said that I could feel my heart pounding faster at the mere thought of getting a chance on that brand new shiny red swing. Before I knew it, I was swinging my legs over the top of her Uncle Henry's prize camellia bushes, heading for the red swing.

It was wonderful.

The wind rushed by my face, tickling my ears as I pumped my legs. I wanted to go higher and higher. Each time I came down, the ground rushed to meet me in an indistinguishable blur. Each time I went up, I pumped harder. I wanted to go high enough to get close to heaven. I thought maybe Mama and Daddy could see me and know I was all right.

As the swing cleared the tree tops, Aunt Meg's voice brought me crashing back to earth.

"Boy, you get down from there this instant! You must've lost your mind. Good thing I got a ride home with Irene. No telling what kind of foolishness you might've tried. Get back over here!" Aunt Meg's face was a peculiar shade of crimson that bordered on purple.

April let me into my yard through the back gate. I didn't dare climb over the fence again. Slowly I made my way to the door where my aunt was standing. The sound of her hand on my cheek shattered the stillness of the summer afternoon. The sting was immediate, and my tears flowed uncontrollably.

I'd never seen Aunt Meg so angry. Her mouth formed a thin red line. Her eyes were flashing fire. When she spoke, her voice was a choked screech. "You will never, I mean never again disobey me on this matter. You are never under any circumstances to go into that man's yard again. You are never to associate with any of that family. Do I make myself clear?"

"Yes Ma'am."

"Now go to your room and don't come back until you're called," she said. She turned her head, but not before I caught the glitter of tears on her own cheeks.

It's been more than twenty years since that afternoon. I've been away a long time. Now I'm back, standing at the same back door, looking over the same fence, into Mr. Henry's back yard. Everything here is exactly the same, and yet nothing is. All of the boxes, newspapers and other clutter have been sent to the dump. The red swing was long ago dismantled and stored away with other childhood memories.

Heather, Ben and Trey have all moved away.

It's summer again. I can almost hear Aunt Meg. "Never, do you hear me?"

Looking around the house one last time, I lock the back door.

"Mark, darling, are you ready to go?" says April. "I dropped Aunt Lois back at home. Uncle Henry's grave looks so pretty since the camellias are in bloom." Her full red lips stretch into a smile as inviting as the long-ago bright shiny red swing.

JAS. MARDIS

Tricky Slim and the Peepers

Son, there was a time when a man would do just about anything to be a bigger man. Such was the case wit an' ol boy we called Tricky Slim. Now, we called him that 'cause he had done went back up there in dem woods—back of Camden and Chidester—up 'round Rapes Edition—and got hisself sold up to the Devil. He done it for the purpose of being able to trick peoples.

Ain't that somethin?

Sold his soul for to be able to pull any trick that come up to his mind.

But you see, he wun't man enuf to make the business of selling his own soul, naw, naw. What it was is that his brother had done been to the crossroads with the black cat and all of that business. Then, Ol' Tricky, he went back up in dem woods and found where the bones had been laid and he dug 'em up. That way, you see, he got his brother's powers that the Devil had exchanged for his soul when he come up dead. And that's just what happened to his brother on that very day. He dropped cold, stone dead right where he was that minute dem bones come up outta the ground! All Tricky had to do was lay them bones back into the ground and hope that nobody come up on 'em.

Ain't that somethin'?

Wanted sumpt'n so bad that he sent his brother's soul straight into the hands of the Devil hisself.

See, what they used to do wuz this: take up a black cat, tom cat was the best, and split his belly open wit a knife to get to his spleen. Then, they'd take an' break it right off so that it wuz sharp. Well, dem ol' boys had some words dey don got from the hoodoo woman to say and they'd say 'em. Well, the ground would commence to shakin' and the wind would grow up real high and that wuz the signal to skin and de-bone the cat. Then, with the cat's bones in one hand an' that spleen in the other they'd say dem words again and put that broken spleen under dey tongues.

Well, if the Devil wanted dey soul—most of the time he'd take 'em up on it—then that spleen bone would poke into the man's tongue and he'd get to shakin' and such like a spasm wuz upon him. Then, they tell me, that ol' bone would split the man's tongue in two parts and hang from between lips. Now, that wuz when the man wuz to say dem hoodoo words and spit the bone and the blood from his mouth onto the ground.

Son, dey tell me—an' I believe it to be true—that where the bone and the blood hit on the ground a great hole opened up. Then, the man would fall to his knees and throw down dem cat bones into it! When that wuz done, dey tell me, the man's tongue would come back into one and the hole would close up without a trace of the land being bothered.

Ain't that somethin'?

Like I say to you, dey tell me an' I ain't got no cause to doubt it.

Well, Old Tricky Slim, he come up under that boy—his brother. I can't right place his name, but he knowed what his brother had done. So, one night he got that boy full of shine—moonshine—and got him to say what part of dem woods held his bones. Then, like I told you, he went back up in dem woods and dug around 'til he come up with the very spot.

You can go down to Chidester this very day and peoples will tell you the same.

Not long after his brother come up dead, Ol' Tricky went to showin' off what he got. He was real good at the hoo-ra, oh, he could fun up on just about anybody. But, he was thin build though, and people didn't take too much from a thin fella. So, Ol' Tricky would get a fella real hot behind the hoo-ra to where he wanted to fight.

Now son, I ain't got no reason to make this into no lie. I seent this wit my own eyes!

This one ole boy, gets up from a table and come at Tricky wit a chair.

Tricky just sat there calm as a babe. He even turned his back and went to swiggin' a drank.

When the boy got hisself 'bout ready to hit Tricky with the chair; trying to go upside his head, it broke into tiny pieces lak it was a toy! Just lak a toy!

Then, that ole boy come back at him wit his fist—an this was a big ole boy—an just as soon as his hand come near Tricky's face, he slipped up and fell to the flo'r! Just lak that!

It's true as I am telling it!

Another time, in that same drankin' place, I seen Ol' Tricky Slim put a stack of silver dollars on the table and say to every man in the place, "First man to move 'em can have 'em!"

Boy, let me tell you, not a one of them silver dollars moved an inch! I tried it myself and they wuz stuck to the table like nuthin' I even seen. But, Ol' Tricky Slim, just to show dat dey wuz not glued or nuthin, every now and again he'd reach up and take one off the top and buy up a round of dranks. Then, he gets up to leave, after all that funning, and puts his hands flat on the table around dem silvers and that little bitty stack of silver dollars, well it growed back up to the big stack dat he had when he sat down there!

Ain't that somethin?

But, you wanna know what Ol' Tricky was knowed all around for doin'? And, you can still find some peoples down home that'll tell you the same. He was knowed for makin' eggs into peepers. You kno' what a peeper is, son? It's a baby chick and Ol' Tricky could make'em appear jus' by waving his hand.

That ain't no lie. He did it to jus' about every man, woman and child dat lived down home! You see, Ol' Tricky would hang 'round the gen'ral sto' and wait for you to come up and get some eggs. Back then you just put the eggs in a paper sack. It want no carton like in the sto' now. Then, you'd take the paper sack up to the counter and Ol' Tricky would come up on ya, "Hey now. Hey now. What yu gon do wit all dem peepers?" And, then he'd give a wave of his hand—like he was swattin at a fly—something like that, yu know. Well, by the time you looked back at that paper sack it would commence to move all about and makin' a sound lak a peeper. Then, just lak that, dem peepers would jump outta that bag and get to running all over the counter and makin a noise!

Then, after a bit, Ol' Tricky would gather up dem peepers and put 'em back in that paper sack. He'd wave his hand a coupla times, and the paper sack would be full of eggs again. Ol' Tricky, he'd be full of laughs.

Well, most folks just stopped buying them eggs when Ol' Tricky wuz up in dat sto'. Some other folks stopped buying 'em all together. Ain't that somethin?

He give up his soul, that Ol' Tricky Slim, just to turn a egg to a peeper and back to a egg.

That Tricky Slim wuz a funner allright, but he been gone for quite a while. Turns out that he wuz up to that sto' one mornin' an had waved his hand over a paper sack for a funnin' on some new gal in town. Well, I heard that the eggs stayed on as eggs that day. Sure did. And that new gal in town she showed Tricky a balled up fist when he come up to see what happened to dem peepers. A balled up fist. Then, they tell me, that she turned her hand over for Ol' Tricky to see what she had in it. He did and he never said another word about what it wuz. Then, just lak that, SNAP!, he dropped dead as a bug! That ol' gal, they tells me—an' I got no cause to doubt it—she just stepped over to Tricky's dead body and stood her ground over him. She had one leg on each side of his head, they say. Then, she say some words what sound lak that hoodoo woman's words. Now, when she done that, they tell me, that the ground beneath her feet and all around Tricky Slim's dead body commence to shake. It shook lak that for a few minutes then, it stopped and the place got real calm.

That gal? Well, she just as quiet as she pleased, stepped back over Tricky's body and strode outta that sto' never to be seen again.

As for what she showed to Tricky Slim that day I don't know for sure. But, I hear that the hoodoo woman been telling folks who ask that she musta showed him one of dem bones. I hear tell it musta been a spleen.

---

* This is a variation of a folktale—or not, that I heard growing up in Arkansas. All apologies to the families of any of the men who went by the nicknames: Tricky-Slim, John, Paul and the other surnames that supplied these tales.

LINDSAY PATTERSON

The Tarnished Hero

Some adolescent experiences are best kept inside the outer reaches of our memories, but try as I might I can never forget the warm September morning Piedmont Jones swaggered into my seventh grade classroom. He looked evil, and next to my magnificently scrawny body, monstrous. He did not, however, turn out to be the big, vicious bully that I and the rest of the fellows in my class had feared. Rather, he immediately took it upon himself to become our friend and mentor.

"Y'all not mens, just babes," Piedmont informed us the afternoon a rain squall sent us racing into the small, smelly room marked "Boys," where he announced that he, and only he, had the right equipment to satisfy a woman and dared us to compare his "thing" with ours. When comparisons were made, we all agreed that what Piedmont possessed was so out of the ordinary that it just might be "unique."

After that, Piedmont regularly and enthusiastically checked our development, but never once offered us any real encouragement. But to keep our hopes high he shared with us his own prodigy's activity by naming names and giving times and places. He even showed us prophylactic evidence and dramatized in words and pantomime his passionate moments.

Our seventh grade teacher, however, had, after the second week of school, publicly "washed" her "hands" of Piedmont. He never came to class on time or opened a book or answered a question and sat most of the day dozing or snoozing. Yet, he became our hero the day she ordered us to hold out our left hands and receive two hard taps from her thick wooden paddle. But when she reached Piedmont he snatched the paddle from her grasp and, in a voice so resplendent with evil that it made all of us shudder, forbade her to "ever touch" him unless she wanted "to see the blackest side of midnight."

Later, Piedmont explained that no women had ever "hit" him, including his "own momma." And in the schoolyard that became our shibboleth whenever we, too, were threatened: "Not even my own momma hits me!" we would snarl, even though everyone knew that our mothers still did—whenever and wherever they pleased.

Although Piedmont never asked or demanded anything of us, we gladly paid him tributes by giving him our pennies, nickels and bologna sandwiches. He, in turn, protected us and showed us how to protect ourselves, but most important of all, taught us about revenge and honor and how no "man" ever lets an insult go unchallenged, especially from a woman.

Of course not all of us believed that Piedmont was perfect, and, if actually put to the test, could walk on water. He had narrow slits for eyes and a black mole on his left cheek, and another larger one covering his Adam's apple, birthmarks which some us thought indicated a serious flaw in his character.

But on a blustery January morning all of us cheered lustily when Piedmont arrived in class on time and in high, good humor. He clutched a brown paper bag as though it contained his life, and as he swaggered toward his desk, let it be known that we were to meet him in the john at first recess.

In the john, Piedmont sat on a window ledge with his legs crossed and a sly glint in his "China men's eyes," and the brown bag resting gently on his lap. But he would not open the bag until all of us had quieted down, and when all of us had, he tantalizingly withdrew a pale pink object. Everyone was stunned, and those of us who had never touched such an object before, struggled for air.

"Who was she?" all of us wanted to know.

"Real gen-yoo-wine silk!" Piedmont smirked.

"But who was she?" we asked again, this time in unison.

That, Piedmont asserted, would be too dangerous for any of us ever to know. He winked, and that's when we realized what he had all along wanted us to realize—the woman had been rich and white. Our admiration for Piedmont soared.

That spring Piedmont became the star outfielder on our school's softball team, and thus, something of a local celebrity. His new status, we, his staunchest admirers were pleased to note, did not go to his head. He still bragged about his conquests while disabusing us of the notion that we, too, would soon become "real men." But on the last day of school Piedmont "saw" in our bleak futures hope, for on the spur of a teary-eyed moment, we had all been invited by our classmate Barbara to play football on her family's farm. If we were delighted by the invitation, Piedmont was overjoyed. He knew the farm well, he said, and he knew, too, that Barbara's folks would be nowhere in sight and that it would be the perfect opportunity for us, his "babes," to prove our mettle as men.

The farm was conveniently located on the northern edge of town, and its farmhouse was nestled picturesquely beneath a clump of impressive oaks a short distance from the main highway. Behind the farmhouse lay a huge, open field and a grove of tall pine trees and, as we slowly filed into our classroom to receive our final report cards, Piedmont cheerfully briefed us on strategy.

After the softball game each "babe" was to invite a girl to go strolling into the pine grove. We could invite anyone except Janie D., a plain, big boned girl with a puppy dog personality who had never uttered an unkind word to anyone and, probably never would have, except that when Piedmont grabbed her hand and tried to pull her into the pine grove she flatly refused to budge.

Several girls had already strolled into the heavily wooded area and disappeared from view, but upon realizing the intentions of their escorts had quickly returned to the open field. Janie must have noticed this too, for she had abruptly started toward the farmhouse when Piedmont tripped her form behind and pinned her to the ground. Screams saturated the hot, summery air.

"Please somebody, help!" Janie cried, but almost everyone had panicked and scattered to the outer reaches of the open field. Only I stood begging Piedmont "to get up and let Janie go!"

"Hold her legs!" he ordered, as he ripped open her dress and she lay naked except for an elastic band that had held up her white homemade undergarment.

I could see the hurt and humiliation in Janie's eyes as I went to grab Piedmont around the neck. But no sooner had I touched him than he sprang up like a frightened jackrabbit and streaked toward the pine grove, for no one else had spotted the well-dressed man speeding past the farmhouse into the open field until Barbara—the classmate who had invited us to the farm—shrieked.

"Uncle!" she cried.

"You there!" the man puffed after Piedmont, but he was too late. Piedmont, his brown muscular body glistening in the afternoon sun, had quickly disappeared from view.

The man, it turned out, was indeed Barbara's uncle and gruffly ordered all of us to write down our names and addresses and then to "go" at once to our "respective homes" and "wait for the proper authorities."

But none of us had ever heard the term "the proper authorities" before and were at a loss as to who it really meant. I spent the remainder of the afternoon in my room with the door locked and my desk and bed pushed up against it. But no one came by, and that night I went with my father and brother to our high school's commencement ceremony, which was being staged that year at St. John's, the big, rambling clapboard church that always looked as if it would one day collapse under the weight of salvation.

I sat in the balcony with Hamp and Freddy, who had been at the farm that afternoon too. But unlike the rest of us, Freddy had the presence of mind to sign a fictitious name and address and was still bragging about it when the music started and a door opened beside the pulpit and out walked the commencement speaker that the program notes identified as the president of a small Texas college. Both Hamp and I slumped as far down in our seats as we could get, for there was no mistake about it, he was the exact same man who had puffed after Piedmont. And when it came his turn to speak he wasted no words of flattery on the graduates and their academic achievement as previous speakers had done but, wanted to know who, if anyone, had paid any attention to their moral development. He paused, as though waiting for some sort of collective audience response, but there was no sound, only the whirl of the overhead plantation fans; and then he went on to recount in dramatic detail what he had witnessed on the farm that afternoon.

"I have their names right here!" he fairly boomed and plucked from his inside coat pocket the sheaf of white papers all of us had scrawled our names on.

The audience sat in stunned and unaccustomed silence; I closed my eyes and prayed: "I will always take my hat off in the presence of ladies and open doors for them and give them my seat when there are no seats, just like my father has always told me to do," I mumbled. "And I will never-never-never ever try to do anything to them that they don't want me to do. So, please help me, because I don't have to tell you how crazy my father is or what he is liable to do when he hears my name read. So, you've got to help me, please!"

"If I ever hear of anything like this again," the man, who had a deep mellifluous voice, was saying now, "I will come back from Texas and personally see that all-of-them are prosecuted to the fullest extent of the law. You got my word on that! He drawled, then carefully folded up the sheaf of white lined sheets with our names on them and returned it to his inside coat pocket.

Hamp grinned and smacked me on the arm.

"I got to go!" I said, suddenly jumping up and going out of the church.

Outside, a soft mist was falling, for which I was grateful, since men weren't supposed to cry and, if they did, no one was ever to know about it. Piedmont had taught me that. But I shuddered when I thought of how my father would surely have come bounding up into the balcony the instant he heard my name and, in front of everyone, would have given men the whipping of my life. It would have been an humiliation from which I am certain I would have never recovered.

In the back seat of our car I promptly fell asleep and did not awake until my father turned off the main highway onto the graveled street that led to our house.

"What do you know about that business on the farm this afternoon?" he asked.

"He's asleep," said my brother.

"I'll bet," sighed my father with a weariness that told me he would never again bring up the subject. Nor did he, and nor did I ever see Piedmont again after that. But it was rumored that during one of the many revivals in our town that summer, he had gotten saved.

CLIFTON L. TAULBERT

The End of a Season

The colored people of Glen Allan were close friends and many were related. When sickness invaded their ranks they would find time to comfort each other, and they'd sit up at night with each other without giving thought to the day of labor ahead.

During sickness, the women would sit for hours talking, sharing memories, recalling their past and the pasts of others. It was during these times that I learned much about our family, our history and where we had come from.

As I remember the illness of my great-grandmother, I recall her many friends and how they all came to sit with her. They came to comfort. They came to visit.

It was the end of the season and we had picked the last of the cotton. Only a few plantations had scraps left, and just about everybody in Glen Allan had put their sacks away for the year.

The leaves had fallen off the big pecan tree and all the chinaberries had been gathered for the fires used to smoke the winter's meat. Ma Ponk had not raised hogs this year, so we had no need to keep the chinaberries, but as always, we stocked up on the cut wood, logs and coal. For the last month, Ma Ponk had been spending her evenings and Saturdays taking care of my great-grandmother, Mama Pearl. This Saturday, however, Ma Ponk didn't go around to Mama Pearl and Poppa's house, the "big house," mainly because we had to get in the coal and wood. Usually Ma Ponk would be full of talk, trying to get me to work harder, but not this Saturday. In fact, she had not been herself for days. She was worried about Mama Pearl. Ma Ponk had said if Mama Pearl didn't get well before winter, she doubted that she'd make it.

We worked fast, or at least Ma Ponk did. I was not yet six, too young to be of much help. We did little talking. Ma Ponk had me bundled up to keep out the chill but as she worked she seemed not to notice me. We finally finished moving the coal from the front yard to the coal house. After finishing, we went in and Ma Ponk warmed up some leftover chicken wings and rice. She fixed our plates and took them to the front bedroom. We would always eat there at dusk so we could look out the window and see all the comings and goings. After finishing our food, we sat in silence in a room lighted only by the flames from the wood stove. Ma Ponk sat in her rocking chair, rocking back and forth and looking through the limbs of the big pecan tree, straining to see Mama Pearl's roof. Occasionally she would hum her father's favorite hymn, "Precious Lord," as we both just sat in the darkness watching the night slowly come into our lives.

There was no rush to undress. We sat ready to go. Ma Ponk could be counted on to be there for Mama Pearl if she needed her tonight.

I curled up on the foot of the big iron bed and watched Ma Ponk. While lying down partially asleep, I saw her stand up and move quickly to the front door. She had seen her Cousin Beauty walking toward her house.

"Ponk, it's me, Beauty. Pearl ain't well at all. In fact, Elder Young wants us to sit up with her till Dr. Duke come."

"All right, Beauty," Ma Ponk said. "I just knew that Ma Pearl was gittin' no better."

"Lord, chile," said Ma Ponk, looking over at me on the bed, "I sho hate to git you out in this cold, but we better go."

While Cousin Beauty waited by the wooden gate, Ma Ponk got her heavy coat, a small can of Garrett snuff and her spit cup, blew out the lamp and made ready to leave.

With the darkness, the old pecan tree by the public water hydrant looked massive and scary. We walked as fast as we could, our silence interrupted only by the sound of the gravel under our feet and a whistling of wind through the pecan branches. As we passed Mr. Stanley's shotgun house, Mrs. Stanley called from her front door. "Ponk, how is Miss Pearl? I hear she got worse about an hour ago. Ya'll call me if you need me. I'll be home."

I could see Mama Pearl's house as we got closer. The front steps were tall and wide. The house had been built after the flood of 1927, so the foundation was built off the ground. Ma Ponk went in first and we followed. The front room, nicely furnished with black leather couches and chairs, was filled with people just sitting and waiting. As we walked in, Ma Ponk's presence was acknowledged. I quietly listened, too young really to understand, as the other people explained the situation. I looked from face to face. No one was smiling. They talked and nodded their heads. I curled up in Poppa's big chair. I wanted to see Mama Pearl, but I didn't say anything. I felt alone in the crowded room. From Poppa's big chair I could look into the small bedroom each time someone went in or came out of Mama Pearl's room. The small bedroom off the living room had always been my favorite place. It was cherry and I loved sitting on the big brass bed with the soft mattress. Mama Pearl would let me take my naps there. Tonight, however, there was no laughter in that room, only silent sadness. The normally bright room was dim and the pretty spread was gone, with quilts in its stead. As the hour grew later I watched the faces grow more solemn. My relatives and friends of Mama Pearl continued going in and out the small bedroom.

"She won't last the night," Cousin Beauty said as she walked out.

Ma Ponk wasn't much for talking or passing opinions. She just sat by the wood stove and rocked. It was a cold night, but the big iron heater kept the front room cozy and warm. Everyone sat in a semi-circle around it, making sure there was a big spit can in the middle.

As they sat and talked, Ma Ponk came over and put a quilt over me where I lay curled up in Poppa's big chair. Occasionally someone would get up and check on Mama Pearl. The rest of the time, we all listened to Miss Sue, a ninety-year-old colored lady who remembered much about our families' lives. Miss Sue talked about General Wade Hampton coming into the Delta to set up his plantation after the Civil War. She also recalled the arrival of my great-grandfather, Sidney Peters, into the Delta with his half-Jewish wife, Miss Rose.

"Yeah, Ponk, I sho knowed your people. Course, I wuz just a girl, but I 'member when Sid and Rose Peters come up from the hills. Yor Pa had a fine carriage, pulled by a team of white horses. He was the blackest colored man I'd seen, and Miss Rose, well we all thought she wuz white. Yes, Miss Rose's Jewish folk lived down by Mayerville."

Ms. Sue probably would have continued to talk about Ma Ponk's grandparents, but Cousin Beauty interrupted her. "Sue, what happened to Ole man Josh Wade's boy?"

"Well, after his colored mama died, Mr. Josh sent him North. He never came back. Course, you know, mostly all dem real high yallers went North and passed for White. Course, once you pass, you can't come back round again."

They must have talked for hours or listened as Miss Sue talked about the old folks, long since dead. As the conversation continued into the night, I dozed off. But when I awoke, I remember a flurry of activity. Ma Ponk was sitting on the side of the bed wiping Mama Pearl's head. I could see fully into the room now; the door was wide open. There was Mama Pearl, not saying a word, just looking, as if through the ceiling. I could hear her sniffling, and bits of conversation.

"It's her heart."

"Pearl knew it all the time."

"She told me at church 'bout a week ago that she felt she was giving her last covenant."

"But Pearl's all right, she got good religion."

We could hear Ma Ponk talk as she wiped the perspiration.

"Now Mama Pearl, you'll be all right. Hold on 'til Dr. Duke gets here."

Dr. Duke was white and the town's doctor. He took care of the coloreds and the white. And no matter the time, he would come. But before he got there I heard Mama Pearl cry out, "I'm leaving ya'll, the angels are coming to get me." Ma Ponk, through tears, said, "Don't say that. You'll be all right." But this time Mama Pearl couldn't be coaxed back to life. She was tired—her heart was tired. It was the end of her season.

Except for the sound of crying, the small room was still. Mama Pearl was loved by everybody, but she was gone. Just as the leaves had left the pecan trees and the blue sky turned gray, her life had passed into the night. But Ma Ponk was strong. She told everyone to meet her at the house in the morning, so the bedclothes could be washed and the house cleaned. After they left, Ma Ponk was silent as she went into the room, combed Mama Pearl's hair and straightened the bed.

We waited with Poppa for the funeral-home people. After a few hours of sad silence, they came, arranged for the wake and the funeral, and took Mama Pearl's body away. I watched as Poppa closed the door to the room. I saw his tears, and I knew tears meant sadness. Ma Ponk put on her coat, got her spit cup and we told Poppa good night. While we were leaving, Saint Mark's church bells began to toll. Another soldier was gone.

(Excerpt from *When We Were Colored*)

LUVENIA FEARS-PORCHIA

Uncle Tom's Head

The night winds blew against the shotgun house so hard that Rosie and her sister, Mal, thought that someone might be knocking. Last month, someone knocking at this hour would have been okay. Uncle Thomas would rise from the feather bed, grip the long handle shotgun and step to the door frame with a loud holler, "Yeah?!" Then, with little more than a quick stomp of his foot, he'd remove the heavy wood block that stretched from floor to ceiling across the door and check out the visitor. The wind blew again and the knocking returned. This was not last month. Uncle "Tom" would not be rising from the puffy feathered mattress. The long handle of the gun would not be resting against his barrel chest and the bellowy comfort of his holler would not reverberate the wooden timbers of the shotgun house tonight. The knocking winds let loose the verse of fears in the girls from Uncle Tom's recent death from dropsy.

Rosie heard the creaking wood of the door being opened and awoke to sunlight sneaking into the room. Big Mama rested the long wood block against the door frame and flung in the new day. A strong breeze quickly filed past her and chased around the three tiny rooms of the house. "Mo'ning Tom," Big Mama greeted the spirit of her husband like this every morning and every morning it seemed to be Uncle Tom's familiar nose tickles that woke the girls. Rosie tried to nudge Mal awake, but the younger girl was already humming along with the tune that Big Mama was starting to sing.

". . . I once was lost, but now I'm found . . ."

Mal got up and turned back to the small framed bed to make it up. Rosie waited for the cool morning air to chase across her nose, a tickle of sorts, like Uncle Tom's morning call. Instead, the wind merely circled the small room around her. Mal tugged at the sheet while Rosie watched

Big Mama swing back and forth in the doorway. Her eyes were closed and her song never rose above a low whisper. The tail of her nightcoat hung and swayed along with her rhythm and the steady breeze wafting through the open door. Big Mama stopped singing and began conversing with the bright daylight and wind.

Now, Mal tugged at the lightweight crazy quilt and bedsheets until Rosie finally rolled out onto the floor. Together they made the bed and walked the few steps to where Big Mama stood, still talking to the morning, but mingling in bits of her song. "Girls, y'Uncle Tom says Good Mo'ning." Together the girls smiled into the daylight and slowly spoke back their greeting, "Good Mo'ning Uncle Tom."

Tom Moore had been dead for almost an entire month. The girls had come to live with him and his wife almost four years to the date of his death from the only thing that he could not battle and win. Luelle, their mother, was away. She had left them, Rosie 5 and Mal 3, with Rozena and Tom Moore for the short while that she would be gone. Rozena, her aunt, had raised her while her mother was away, now she was needed again. Arkansas had always been hard on the women of this family and the ravages of 1937 Southern racism were even harsher. The girl's father would never see them blossom into their womanhood. There would only be the memory of them; asleep in the darkened room lit by a simple candle's light. The night rider's carving his name in the trunk of an old oak outside the shotgun house meant that he would have to leave Chidester.

Tom Moore and his wife had decided not to have children. For him, these two girls had come to mean everything, especially as his life closed in on him. His legs had begun to swell, slightly at first, then the pus had come, followed by the pungent odor. By then, he knew the illness of the veins was upon him. It had claimed his mother's father and was known to his family as a disease that skipped a generation. Tom had believed the curse to be broken, having already reached his forty-ninth birthday. For years he and Rozena had burdened themselves with their decision to not pass it along to the next generation, since he had not been infected. Now, they allowed themselves the pleasures of parenting, even as their bodies began to peak.

Before dropsy set in, Tom Moore had run with the girls and showed them the ways of the deep, Arkansas woodland that surrounded their township. He had taught them the ways and powers of both the spirit world and of the Lord. Tom Moore had the gift, some called it, to move things at his will. He did not always use this gift, but he wanted to pass along the knowledge that a reliance on and a trust in the land held sway with the spirits. At night they prayed, as a family, for a solid hour amid the haunting sounds and shrieks from the woods. Tom Moore taught the girls to listen for the rhythms within the night sounds. "Listen," he would say, "there is nothing out there tonight that was not there all through the day. Some day I will be gone from this earth, but I will always be with you. Listen for me in the wind and look for me in the light." His love for the girls was honest and brooding. At times it seemed as though they had always been his and Rozena's children.

The morning burst over the hanging clouds and suddenly the girls and Big Mama were awash in a heavenly light. Big Mama hugged the girls close to her and announced that they would be going back to church that morning.

It had been almost a month since Tom Moore had been laid to rest. A rough month of missing and sorrow and learning to brave the nights of aloneness for all three of them. Church had come to their house so that the strain of the long walk would not further burden the family. That was the first week. Early in the second week their small house had the company of the Saints and mourners. Now, in the third week, no one would be coming to worship with them until after the service was completed. Even then it would be the second Preacher or the head Deacon coming by to *check up on things*. So, with the church day already well into the service, Big Mama got the girls dressed and headed up the tracks to the Chidester Baptist Church.

The way to the church was along the tracks, as was the way to everything in Chidester. Large openings in the long stems of grass signaled a new pathway or the clearing before a neighbor's house. The grass was high and the terrain gouged out because the tracks had been laid by prison camp laborers. The prisoners, often made to go into areas that guards would never enter, would dig out hiding holes that they could escape to later. The grass hid them by day and disguised their movement by night. During the daylight hours these tracks were safe to travel, but at the darkest hours they held great dangers for anyone who ventured their dark pathways. Chidester was primarily a black township and many of the escapees were known to lay low there longer than at any other stretch along the way to freedom.

When church ended for the afternoon, Big Mama and the girls were engulfed with fellowship offers. Thinking of the hour, they chose to visit with a neighbor that lived near their clearing along the tracks. It was a good visit filled with the love and companionship that would grow the small township into a great, little city someday. But, the hours passed so quickly that Big Mama missed the leaving hour that would have gotten her and the girl's home before the dark hour set in. By the time she looked out of the small window that was set high on the house wall, the sun was already rimmed to the bottom edge of its sill. She quickly gathered the girls and they set off toward home with the setting sun at their backs.

The clearing that lead to their house from the tracks was a half hour walk from the house where they had been visiting and Big Mama let the girls know that the sun would be down before they reached home. Chidester nights, the girls knew, were like walking into a closet with a blindfold on. They looked now at their feet and counted the number of steps between each of the wooden railroad ties. To step onto the tie would have slowed them down with a stumped toe or an occassional trip. Within a few minutes they had developed a rhythm that missed the ties and walked through the dirt.

Not long after that warning to the girls the fading sun's light at their backs made a thin trace of their shadows as they walked. Soon after that, their footsteps over and through the wood rail ties were the only recorder of their movement. Each step into the two feet of dirt between railroad ties sifted puffs of dirt onto their shoes. Then, with an uncanny rhythm, the three of them, stepped over the wooden tie and back into the dirt.

All around them the high grass swayed and whipped with the small gusts of night winds. Big Mama looked down at her hands, or where she knew her hands to be, and saw nothing as they moved over and through the tracks. She knew that at the end of her arms, attatched to her hands were the girls, Rosie and Mal; but the deep, moon and starless, Chidester night took away all of her sight. She held the girl's wrists, not their hands, for a better grip and would occasionally tighten her grip until the girls complained, but mostly she kept them walking through the darkness.

Big Mama figured them to be another five minutes from the clearing that lead to their home, so she slowed her pace and relaxed her grip. It was then that the wind rose up. The long stems of grass and weeds began to clatter under the fierce blowing. Above them, the sky filled with the flutter of wings. They neither saw or heard birds while around them a stale emanation swelled. The girls clung nearer to Big Mama's legs, still pacing over the tracks, but shaking now. She listened. Again, the wind grew up around them returning a gaunt fear. Big Mama heard, amid the blustering wind, the faint sound of a chain being dragged. She listened deeper into the night and again, the chain resonated between gusts of wind. Over a tie and into the dirt. Over. Into. Over, then slowly into the dirt. Someone for sure was behind them.

Big Mama pushed the girls from her legs and pointed them straight away up the track. "Move it, chillun. Move it, now," the urgency and alarm of her actions and from her voice rekindled their previous rhythm: step, step, rise; step, step, rise. Together, their steps shifted through the dirt and over the wooden ties as if they could see the other's feet. Behind them, the chain drug and dropped over the ties and into the dirt with a renewed urgency. But Big Mama stayed calm kept the girls moving. She whispered, "Move it, now girls. Move it, now."

From the clarity of sound Big Mama knew that the clearing was just ahead. It was in the way that the grass ceased its whistle. It was a lack of sound from up ahead that signaled the opening. It was the knowledge of the land and of the darkness over all of her years that gave her this bearing. She listened again, through the wind and the calmed whipping of the tall grass, and could not hear the dragging chain coming up from behind them. Nothing, and now the winds were suddenly calm and the grasses were suddenly still and the shrieks and croaks of the night animals were suddenly silent. Big Mama led the girls from the tracks and wooden ties onto a footpath of stones that sloped into a smooth, clear course.

Soon, they were standing on the porch of the small house and Big Mama felt the door frame for the iron lock. When she opened the door the room was as dark as the outdoors, but safer. She lead the girls into the room and, closing the door, anchored them against it. In a moment the room was afire with the light of a match, then a candle, followed by the shine of an oil lamp. Big Mama ushered the girls off the door and reached for the long plank that held the door secure. With the door latched and barred, she turned her attention to the girls and warming the house. She motioned the girls to her side and held them as she prayed and thanked the Lord. It was a moment or so later when Big Mama realized that no kindling had been cut that day. They had left for church in such a rush that the day's chores had gone undone. She would have to venture back into the darkness to break up a log or two for a fire.

The house was small, like all the houses, but Tom Moore had spurned the simple "shotgun" design. Instead of the straight-through style, he had put the back door on the side of the house, just off the kitchen area. In front of that door, flush against the wall, was the eating table and that is where Big Mama put the lattern so that its light would shine through the open door while she chopped. The girls sat on the high step in the doorway until Big Mama had broken up some twigs for kindling and called them to carry it into the house. She loaded their tiny arms with the twigs and strips of wood then sent them the few steps back into the house. And, as children do, the girls devised a race for those few steps to the doorway. Rosie and Mal giggled and ran to the three, small steps that led into the doorway and the house. Big Mama decided to break up two more logs for the morning's fire and left the girls to their game.

As the older woman rose her axe the girls became wedged in the small frame of the door. Their kindling caught on the heavy frame making a squeeze-tie of their race into the house. Big Mama chopped the crooked branch that lay on the cutting stump and bits of tree bark flew through the air. When a few flecks of bark hit the giggling girls they stopped wrestling and looked back at Big Mama to frown their complaint. It was when they turned back to their race into the house that they first saw what they would never forget. It was in that moment that Rosie and Mal began their belief of Uncle Tom's words and warnings and promises.

It was then, as they rejoined their task of carrying kindling into that house filled with light from the lattern atop the eating table, that they truly knew how powerful the spirit-world could be. Beside the lattern, on the eating table in plain and illuminated sight, a mere six feet in front of their eyes was an empty pie plate. On that pie plate beside the lattern was the apparition of their Uncle Tom's head! His dark-red skin as clear as the first day they had come to live in that house. His heavy mustache as black as the night itself. His eyes as brown and clearly visible as if the man himself were before them. Tom Moore's head, perched in the pie plate, beside the lattern that sat on the eating table that was flush against the wall, did not smile. He did not wink. He did not twitch and he did not move an inch. He looked directly at the girls who still stood, kindling in hand, wedged in the door frame. He looked into their eyes and he did not smile or move. They also did not move an inch in their amazement.

It was Big Mama's shrill call to the girls that broke the moment's trance. Her words to them never registered, but it was enough to break their staring. Each girl turned and checked with the other to be sure that they had seen what they had just seen. It was a recognition in the other's stare that confirmed the image. It was also that image of Tom Moore's head beside the lantern that calmed them. He had said to them that he would be in the wind and in the light and that he would return. They had nothing to fear from Tom Moore in apparition. Their hearts swelled with the remembrance of his loving touch. He had not come back to haunt them. Again, the recognition in each of the girl's faces unified their lack of fear of the apparition.

In unison they turned back to the apparition and saw the tin pie plate begin to rise from the table. As it rose, Tom Moore's face smiled. Then, quick as a flash the pie plate rose up and flipped backwards into the wall. Rosie was sure that she had seen the plate go into the wall and called to her little sister, "Mal?" The younger girl did not say a word to acknowledge this certainty made so by the lantern's light. Then, or maybe within a few seconds, the pie plate emerged from the wall beneath the table. Both Mal and Rosie heard the sound. They were sure of that in the same way that they watched the plate fall from the wall onto the floor. They had seen it, together, as one.

This time when they turned away from the lantern on the table and the pie plate on the floor beneath, it was not for confirmation. They turned, dropping the kindling in the door's jamb, toward Big Mama. Their voices rang out, "Big Mama. Big Mama, we just saw Uncle Tom. We saw him, Big Mama!"

Big Mama did not have to hear them twice. She did not have to wonder if this were a game. She knew that if the girls had seen Tom Moore it was a warning. She knew the ways of the spirits and that she should obey the sign. She quickly gathered the shocked girls into her arms, rushed back into the house and bolted the door. She gathered the girls against her bosom and heard their story again and again until they were comforted by the telling. Then, she held them closer and prayed for their safety in the night of wonderment and apparitions and warnings. There was no supper that night and no sleeping alone. From the kindling that had been dropped inside the door a fire was made and the three of them cuddled and comforted each other before it. She listened, although she knew that a greater force was operating around them.

A loud noise, a pounding at the door, shook them awake and Big Mama could hear a gang of voices coming from beyond the door. She looked up to see bits of lights seeping through the wall. It was morning. The girls, awakened by the shock of the pounding and afraid, began to cry. "Hush, chile, hush," Big Mama comforted the girls, then rose and approached the door. "Yeah? Yeah?!" her voice cut through the cacophony of the pounding. "Is ev'body awlright in der?" a man's voice shouted back a response. "Open the door and let us see that you is awlright!" his voice rang with a cautious demand. The crowd behind him joined in with similiar mumblings and demands, "Open it up!"

Big Mama unwedged the heavy plank from the door and leaned it against the jam. When she opened the door a gang of men rushed inside and surveyed the room. Seeing that she and the girls were all right and alone, they apologized and explained their actions. "Sorry, Ms. Rozena," they began, "but we had two mens killed just about three-hun'ed yards from yo' house. We was just sho that the fellas what killed them boys had come up here and don' the same to you and yo' girls!"

Big Mama motioned the girls to her and turned her attention skyward to the morning sun. When she spoke it was not to the crowd and not as much even to the children. "Thank you, Tom Moore!" her eyes welled. "Tom Moore comed here t'warn us from that danger and that killing. He comed here and showed hisself to these girls when I wuz chopping some kindling in the night!" She held the girls closer and a strong breeze built and chased into the house and surrounded them. Big Mama wanted to tell them that this too was Tom Moore. She wanted to say that he promised to stay and protect them. She wanted to say to the girls that they were loved, but her words did not come easily. For Rosie and Mal whatever she would have said would not have mattered. It would not have meant as much to them, in that moment, as the breeze coming into the crowded doorway. It was a breeze that lifted, then fell cool on their faces in such a way that it tickled their noses.

KAYLOIS HENRY

A Sort of Homecoming

1.

The plane flies low over the island. Out the window on the left-hand side, just beyond the wing I sit next to for superstitious reasons, I glimpse the bay. It's blue, an impossible art film shade. I can see to the bottom, even at that height. Shapes swivel this way and that, while the plants wave welcome like hands.

The mountains just beyond the bay appear to scrape the bottom of the plane. There are houses scattered among the peaks, testaments to faith and ingenuity. They climb the mountainsides, a confused collection of tin-roofed shacks held by slender poles or mere belief, on steep inclines where one push could make domino into the sea. God has sprinkled houses on the mountain, like seeds and grown villages.

A song snippet whirls a moment in my mind. *I will live on by the side of the road, on the side of a hill . . .*

The air is alive here, a large dripping creature that always follows too closely. Off the plane, it follows at my heels, panting on my neck. The backs of my clothes are already damp as I wait for my luggage full of lighter clothes to come off the carousel.

A shuttle bus takes me and other guests from the airport to the all-inclusive hotel on the beach. The road is one of the few paved, and yet it still rattles the bones like beads as the bus barrels through the busy streets. I want to crane my neck out the window and stare at everything, like a tourist. I *am* a tourist this time.

Inside the hotel, porters take the bags. Their skin is browner than my own, sun-loved. I've lived too long without sunshine. I shake off the thought. Instead, I think of the sunblocks I have.

"Don't come back too black," friends advised. I bought the highest SPF rating I could find, despite the cashier's puzzled look.

The hotel has stepped from the world of the travel brochure. It is a six-story building gleaming pink and sparkly in the bright Caribbean sunshine. Its name says it all: Club Paradise. Palm Tree-lined walkways, terrazzo-filled lobby with hanging and potted plants, rattan chairs with tropical print cushions and matching glass-top tables. The hushed clap of my sandals on the floor strikes the right travel tone. This is how a visitor sounds when she walks through the lobby of a hotel in the Caribbean. Quiet.

2.

My dreams are shadow and smoke at the mercy of the slightest force. I often dream of quicksand traps and tumbleweeds, but the places always change. I have never had the same dream twice. In my waking life I am equally rootless: four jobs in four years in four different cities since I left home and school. My grandmother says I am cursed with a wanderer's soles, the consequence of a mother who went too far from home too soon. Grandma has never moved beyond the five miles of her small island village, save to visit that same daughter thousands of restless and cursed miles away. And that daughter, my mother, has never moved beyond her adopted city, save when her soles itch for native sand.

I have come to find roots here.

My hotel room is on the fourth floor. There are French doors that open to a tiny balcony. I can see the bay from there, smell the salt and the sea. The air is still and windless.

At the gates of the hotel, I see more sun-loved people gather outside, sitting on boulders and rip-rap jutting from the water. They cleave the stillness with their voices, which sound like singing. I know they are speaking their own English, barely discernible from the one my ears have grown used to. Their voices float up; a collective call to me. The bottoms of my feet begin to itch.

The woman who shares my room is named Karen. *Car-rin* she pronounces it. She says she's an industrial engineer from Augusta, Georgia, and isn't this just the most beautiful place in the world. She has an excited way of speaking, none of those languid country tones. I think she has tried very hard to disguise her countryness. Words give her away. She says *bay-yack* for back, and *strimp* for shrimp, but her secret will be safe with me. We all need our secrets.

I tell her the island is haunted and that a spirit tries to go home with each tourist, slipping into a suitcase or infusing the soles of shoes. She laughs, "Looks like you have already been inhabited by a local spirit," she says, pantomiming drinking from a glass.

The white people are the obvious ones here. There is nowhere for them to blend in and hide. Their very skin brands them sightseers. Still, some make the attempt. They don the tri-colored knitted caps, allow their stringy hair to be braided. They dance libidinously, as they think the locals do. They saunter in sandals, ragged short and t-shirts and go on about culture and vibes. I understand them, their need to try to feel less foreign. But I envy those who make no concession. Their inelegance, arrogance, as well as skin, marks them as tourist: noses shielded with cream or plastic, the Banana Republic safari clothes in crisp, new beige, bright colored flip-flops or sandals with socks, the desire for hamburgers rather than curry. There is no mistaking them, no confusion.

The rock people become more animated when the whites come by. The languid sing-song changes into a fierce flying hawking. "Oranges! Nice, nice oranges. Fresh from Mamma's grove!" "Beads of loove! Wear dem and get you 'earts desire!" "Braids missus! Braid you 'air nice, nice." A woman takes the offer for braids. The other braiders gather around, giving advice, flattery, peddling more to the white woman. The dark hands work meticulously, scooping and separating the blond hair, like coal in pyrite, braiding it quickly into golden lengths of cord.

Karen comes to see what I am looking at. She snorts under her breath as she watches the white woman get her hair braided and the white men buy trinkets. "I'll be damned if I let one of them touch my hair." Karen's hair is a curly perm that frames her elfin face like an oily cloud. "But then, they wouldn't ask us." She winks at me with that comment, our mutual brownness unspoken. Yes, but what *will* they ask us?

3.

Club Paradise's printed motto is *All the fun, none of the worry*. There is, however, another one in smaller print that is much more difficult. *Experience the island without leaving home*. Both are fairly easy to see. The hotel includes everything it can behind its high fenced walls: Sports, wind-surfing, sun-bathing, para-sailing on the private beach (dutifully patrolled by men in white uniforms). And for those of us more adventurous, there are the planned trips. Today Karen and I decide to go shopping.

Karen likes to shop. Her clothes are immaculate, understated, and reek of expense. She spends more than an hour putting the day's look together, carefully preparing the canvas of her body for each great unveiling. Preparations include showering, layering the scent (*Anais Anais*, I believe) and fastidiously ironing all the day's clothes, including underwear.

I look down from the balcony. The people who sit on the rocks wear polyester, skirts, shirts and pants. All ill-fitting, second-hand-looking clothes that have never seen an iron. The women wrap their heads in shabby scarves. They don't look very different from Karen and I. So skin won't be too advantageous here. I think of my travel clothes. I will still look like a tourist.

The hotel bus jostles its way through the busy traffic of the city's downtown. The logo on the side is a magnet for the street hawkers. They clamber through traffic to the bus. They hold their wares to us, like offerings. They catch sight of me and their pleas turn familial. "Sistah, sistah, buy a jew box! Match you 'at. Hey sistah, buy some beads. 'elp you brutha, sistah. Loovly purse to match you loovly 'art. sistah, help . . ."

I am impassive to the pleading. The sun-loved faces fade before me. Instead, I see spiders, crawling and clawing at the windows, spinning webs.

When I was a child, my mother told me the story of a spider. The spider asked a tiger to name something after it. The tiger had the preeminent place in the world, with many things named after it. The spider was a small weak animal, with nothing but its web. Tiger said he would grant spider's wish, if spider would complete two tasks: capture a gourd filled with bees and bring him a large snake, alive. Of course the wily spider did so, tricking the bees into flying into the gourd and getting the snake to follow him on pretense of gift. So now all the island stories bear the spider's name, Anansi.

Spiders inhabit the souls of the folks here. That is how they survive on so little—how they are able to live in the world full of white and brown tigers—by being clever.

The hotel has made sure that its guests only see the best parts of the island, so we are shuttled to the exclusive high street in the center of the city. The shops sell everything you could find back home (duty-free, of course) with some island flourishes. Things are brighter and gaudier, screaming tropicality and the "I went to the islands" message that tourists like bringing back. The hawkers are at a minimum here. On the high street most of the people look like tourists shopping. The shop assistants are clean, well-dressed (no polyester in sight) and friendly, as if they too know they are part of the displays.

I see the others on the edges, though—their baskets on heads, their synthetic clothes—scuttling on the corners, scurrying away into the alleys along the street. The high street has pushed them from the picture until they seem only a fleeting glimpse out of the corner of my eye. I see filaments of webs in the debris: discarded clothing, orange husks, scattered beads, all at seemingly random intervals. I can see the pattern, forming the outer ring, leading away and center.

I move to follow the lines, but Karen grabs my arm. What do you think of this? She is holding up a pair of bright earrings, in a crazy pattern of twisted silver. They're lovely, I tell her. Just lovely.

At night I sit on the balcony listening to the bay waves crash against the rip-rap. I remember watching a National Geographic special about how spiders can survive in extremes that would kill mammals.

4.

Postcard to: Katie MacKenzie, 7 Cheetwood Ave., Kingston.

(Picture of several small waterfalls. People climb them. They are scantily clad.)

Hey Ms. Mac! Mummy gave me your address and said I should contact you when I arrived. So here I am. Well. I'd forgotten how much it smells here. It's a sort of unwashed funk that fixes itself in the nostrils and just doesn't move away. The only time it stops is when I reach the inside gates of the hotel. Then all I smell is coconut and limes. It has been years since I've seen you. I realize how little I know—about you, Mum, the land. How can you grow cassava next to tangerines?

How do the houses cling to the mountain air? Can people see me? I won't see you. Too far away.

Love.

P.S. Do the spiders here bite?

Postcard to: Kitty Rose, Eglinton District, Eglington, PA, Manchester.

(Picture of the smiling dark brown face of a woman, fleshy cheeks, wide lips, a colored scarf on her head, and atop that a basket filled with fruit.)

Aunt Kitty. The heat and the dirt here are more than I remember. I keep thinking of Grandma's house and all the red clay and how it would get in all my whitest clothes, never to come clean again. All my clothes came home with a stain, really, no matter how dark they were. It doesn't happen now. I think they have developed tougher detergents. Does Grandma still have chickens? Do you still kill them for Sunday dinner? I'm not sure you'd recognize me now. Nobody does really. I've grown older, and taller and skinnier since you last saw me. I'm not even sure I would recognize you. The woman on the front is how I remember you. Are you still like that? Anyway, take care of yourself.

Love.

I don't send them. Instead, I will send the two postcards the hotel leaves in the writing desk in the room. On the front is a picture of Club Paradise, secure and fresh-smelling in the sunset. On both backs, I write the following:

Hi. In town now, but can't see you. Only here the weekend. The island is beautiful, and so is the hotel. Miss you very much. Mummy and Daddy send their love. Call soon.

Love.

5.

People ask me where I am from.

It happens first when I decide to take one of the hotel's more adventurous tours of an old plantation. Karen turned up her nose. Why on earth would I want to see a plantation? My ancestors saw enough of them up close, thank you very much. So I leave her to the straw market, bartering her way to happiness.

The plantation sits atop a short mountain, or a tall hill. On the way up, the bus passes a group of children walking. They are in their school uniforms—girls in dark skirts, white shirts and red ties, the younger ones in jumper dresses. Their shoes are caked with dust. On their white socks, I see traces of familiar faded red. The busy driver slows and beeps his horn at them. They wave in unison, smiling big friendly native smiles. At the top of the road, I look back down, at spiders where the girls used to be.

Zita Jones, the tour guide at Long Hill Road Plantation, gives us a brief history of the land and the area surrounding it. During the talk she looks at me, surreptitiously at first, and later a bit more boldly. The plantation is beautiful. Zita is too, the perfect blending of all the people who have settled on the island. Both dark and light, with a honeyed complexion, wide face, hair kept in a bun. Her natural unruly patois is held at bay by an accent that speaks more of finishing school and college. To see her is to see the world.

I hide from her seeking looks behind my large designer sunglasses, deliberately brash American sun dress and closed-toe sandals. I am a tourist, I chant to myself. I begin to believe it.

"Eh ya, sistah," Zita says to me during a lunch break in the big house.

Huh? I say.

Zita stares perplexed a second then recovers her tour-guide smile. "Oh, I'm sorry. It's just that you look so much like someone I know."

"People tell me that all the time."

"Are you from here? Are your people here?"

I am here on a visit. I won a contest.

Zita says nothing. "Hmm. You have to have some island blood. We can usually tell our own. No matter how far away they are, the island always calls them back to see if they meant it. Perhaps your grandparents?"

"I'm just American. That's all."

Another of the guests approaches to speak with Zita and I escape to the verandah. A band is playing lilting Caribbean music. One of the men plays a wooden box with little metal tines like a fork's that he strums while singing. They look at me and the one with maracas tips his hat. "Mamma look at Booboo/ They shout/ Dey motha tells dem shut up you mouf/ That is your daddy/ Oh no/ My daddy can't be ugly so." I walk into the grass to gaze at the trees—bread fruit with their thin finger leaves, limes, poinsettia, ferns. I feel my feet sink into the red clay.

There is a village of white people, Germans, who live in the hill near the plantation. They are preserved in the same way that villages in National Geographic specials are. Only they are Aryan rather than African. They just look so out of place, these blond, blue-eyed people in the same polyester tatters, speaking in the same sing-song voice. "There are only 125 white people left in Seaford Village," the white, German-Jamaican guide tells us. A row of the children who live in the village come outside their one-room schoolhouse to greet us. There is evidence of racial mixing. They seem so at home here, these last of the white people, like they were being kept in a shabby cage in an equally shabby zoo. One of the white children stares at me and winks.

We end the tour back at the plantation, where we eat roast pig and hear more island music. I listen to the other tourists to take my cue for what to say. An actuary from Arkansas tells someone how lovely and simple things are here. How she would love to retire and move here. Her companion, a stockbroker from Vermont, disagrees: Oh this island is nice to visit but really, it's just so . . . well, Third World. Not so, says the white man in the Rasta cap. They have just learned to live without all the material bourgeois possessions that we have grown to depend on so much. In fact I think they are very advanced minority populations. More so than some back home.

The black back-home in me should have bristled, but didn't. I realize I am floating through, I am not "back home," nor am I here. I skirt Anansi's web—I still it—with feigned ignorance as my shield. It is my own creation, forged by distance in the heat of time, shined with apathy and fear. I slice through the threads of understanding and memory as if they were so much flimsy silk.

Yet I feel it fall away under attacks of memory. Auntie Kitty approaches me with a tray filled with pineapple slices. She holds it out to me and stares. My uncles and godfather play in the band. "Back to back/ belly to belly/ I'm not going back/ I done dat already." Grandma scuttles away with the dirty plates and cups into the kitchen. The air has returned and kneads the back of my neck with hot, moist fingers. I close my eyes, shake my head. Chant the Fifty Nifty United States in order. I feel something crawling up my leg. I open my eyes. I crush it.

6.

When my father, Richard, left the island to go to America, he said it was temporary. Jobs were scarce and danger prevalent. The large white mother country had cut the apron strings for her brown child, and it fought and fell as it tried to walk alone. Richard went to America to make money and come back. It was two days after I was born.

I lived with my grandmother, who spoiled me, pinching my cheeks and feeding me. She said I loved the red clay outside the house and was constantly making my way out of the crib to play in the muck. I don't remember any of it.

I remember Opa Locka, USA, where Richard moved his wife and three children two years later. He found a better life clinging to another white mother.

The first time I went back to the island, I was ten. It was the first time I had traveled anywhere on a plane. I remember thinking that it looked just like a National Geographic special. At grandma's house, you had to run into the back and pump a hand pump for about ten minutes to build up water pressure. The house was on a side of a hill, one story in the front, two in the back. Chickens and dogs roamed free. I found myself getting covered in red clay. My aunts and uncles remarked how I had done that as a baby. I thought it was fun.

I used my islandness as a crutch back home, something that made me different from the ordinary Americans. I used to believe if I sprinkled references of it strategically in conversations, I would stand out. Only white people found me exotic. The black ones knew exactly what I was.

The next time I went to the island I was thirteen. I found myself appalled at the conditions and the lack of things to do. I thought the kerosene lamps were stupid and the fire burning in the back of the oil-run refrigerator was a fire hazard. This place was backward and you had to push the hand pump for ten minutes before you could flush the toilet. The aunts and uncles told me how nice and fat I was. I was mortified.

In America, I discovered black consciousness and pride. I wore my hair in braids. I told people that I was an American. On my sixteenth birthday, I stood with 50,000 people in the Orange Bowl Football Stadium in downtown Miami and said the Pledge of Allegiance, making me official. Richard and my brothers flanked me. Joan didn't come.

This is the next time.

7.

At night, I drink to forget my family.

It is the last night for the weekend winners, and the hotel has thrown a great party for us. The house band is playing standard hip-swinging fare and many of the guests have joined in. I sit and down rum, asking my cousin Dwight to pour more. Karen tries to slow my drinking. "You will really hate yourself in the morning."

"I hate myself now," I mumble. "I wish they would just go away."

"Who?" her frustration betrayed in her tone.

"My fucking family!" I gulp the drink. "Can't you see them? They just keep staring at me." I pull at my arms, trying to remove the tiny filaments that keep wrapping around me.

"You need a doctor," Karen says, rising.

I grab her arm. "Please don't go." I watch an uncle pass with a tray filled with nibbles. He glances our way and continues on. I take a deep, rational breath. "I'm just feeling a bit out of sorts, is all." I make my best pathetic smile.

Karen pats my hand. "Okay. I'll come back. But first I must go to the bathroom."

Alone I can't keep my family away. At first they hover on the edges of the room, on the edges of my eyes. But when Karen does not return, they become bolder. Uncle Milton clears the table next to me. Lasell places another rum on my table "Compliments of the gentleman at the bar," he says. I turn to my grandfather, who gives me a wolfish grin and leaves the bar seat. In the glass of rum floats a spider. I try to rise, to run, but I can't. My feet are rooted.

8.

I sit on the balcony of my room listening. It is the next day. Karen has already gone. My bags are packed waiting for me.

I remember Grandpa taking my hand. His touch soft, warm, furry. He holds up my glass. "Drink, mi luv." In his eyes I see nothing but me, his hand and the glass. I feel the spider wriggling as I drink the rum in one gulp.

Inside, I feel it spinning. It's not an unpleasant feeling, sort of tickling in places. In its web are things I chose not to remember, but now will never forget.

I take my bags downstairs and wait for the bus. Grandma passes with a sack of potatoes on her head. She looks at me. I say nothing. The spider spins and spins.

SIGNIFIERS

This final section chases down the signifiers among the Diaspora. From the page they boast with the full barrel chest of sexual noise and cajole the spirit from mouths spilling with despair. They yell and rage against the cacophony that is, sometimes, their lives, and bring the heart to a stuttered halt with belly laughs and midnight jigs. Herein are the offspring of those who still know every verse of *Shine & the Sinking of the Titanic, Stagolee, Dolemite* and the stories of how *Jack b eat the Devil*.

It is here that the corner is revived . . . and the back room, the fishing hole, fish fry and outbacka church whispers that mark a life. What we used to know as the only familiar—a high-cackling voice; the not-long-enough lie; the sexual noise of youth and the sweet-talking trickster—await you . . . again.

VON

send him over

go ahead and nag
let your breasts sag
and your ass drag
tie your head up at night with that rag
send him over

let your stomach pouch
wake up and grouch
keep bitchin every time you open your mouth
make his ass sleep on the couch
send him over

ask him where he's been and where he's goin
constantly accuse him of hoin
tell him the grass needs mowin
and his love needs a lil more showin
send him over

keep cryin like a lil bitch
keep worryin about gettin rich
let him stay horny
don't fuck him in the mornin
listen to your friends
get the last word in
tell him things just aint like they used to be
and send him over
right on over here to me

ashes

don't carve my name in no block of stone
cause this world is definitely not my home
no need to be worried
bout my not being buried
im leavin this place quick fast and in a hurry

get a good nights sleep cause there'll be no wake
no poems and no speeches for my destiny's sake
no funeral home limos
no flower covered caskets
no discussions of how long my funeral lasted

tell the gravedigger to put his shovel away
my body wont take kindly to rot and decay
so when the spirits decide to cancel my lease
strike a match to this temple you label deceased

gather my ashes and when sistuh moon is high
merge my soul with the atlantic sky
like a black butterfly i'll cross the turbulent waters
and return to mother africa her prodigal daughter

SYBIL CANNON

Safe Home

She hurriedly walked down the dirty street toward her two-bedroom apartment. With each few yards the grocery bags she carried became heavier. Using her right knee she hoisted the bags into a better position and shifted the weight against her chest. The movement broke her stride, but she continued to watch her surroundings. She moved cautiously, then fell into her rhythm toward home.

Anxious to get off the street before another neighborhood hoodlum picked her out, she opted for the short cut. The vacant lot teemed with glass shards and trash from the broken bags of trash that served as dinner tables for the homeless and drugged out. She picked her way through the debris: discarded mattresses, heaps of papers, an occasional syringe and the yellowed skin of condoms. She leapt over a muddy patch and landed flush against broken cinder blocks. The hard clumps of mortar hurt right through her cheap shoes. She dismissed the pain and the loss of balance and took another set of steps.

From one side of her face she could see the occasional shadowy form moving between trash heaps. "A rat," she thought, "they keep getting bigger!" A catcall spilled past her ear, then a young woman's voice answered it with a curse. She felt relieved and kept moving.

"There," she allowed herself a sigh as she stepped onto the broken, gray sidewalk at the other end of the shortcut. Her pace slowed by just a step and she turned up the block.

Ahead of her two young men: black, shifting their weight as they walked; pants nearly falling from their sleek, muscular frames, slipped onto the walk ahead. She picked up her pace again, determined to mask the fear that flushed her entire body. She walked right at them without even blinking an eye. She thought of slipping into her crazed mode, but waited for them to make the first move. "I can't be running," her brewing panic was interrupted by the boys' stepping off the walk into the street, surrendering the sidewalk. They passed without so much as a look her way. She swallowed in relief.

Just ahead of her, over the tops of the trees, was the red roof of her apartment building. A smile grew inside and she lifted the heavy grocery bags to her chest. Her arms ached from both the weight and the erratic tensing of her muscles. "Just a bit more," she consoled herself. "Just another block." Thoughts of her simple, but safe little set of rooms added to her feelings of relief. "Home. Just get to the house, chile."

She passed the dilapidated buildings where the boys sold drugs and thought she heard a whisper. She kept moving. Another open space, then another and still another. She thought of the people and the things that happened to them in that darkness. She thought of the potential for fires and how near it would be to her home. "They ought to tear 'em all down!" she reasoned as she passed one of the many people lining the safer end of the block. The unkempt masses of three here or four or five there spotted the corner. "How pathetic. How disgusting," she allowed herself to whisper as she passed the last of the groups.

"Hi, Ruby, girl. How you been gittin' along?" a flashily dressed woman appeared next to her.

Startled, but refusing to show it, she answered, "Oh, hey Minnie. I've been okay. How have you been?" Her bags slipped in her arms.

"Ruby Brown," the woman chewed on the name with the wad of gum in her mouth and swung a red handbag in the air. "Fine, girl, just fine!" She passed Ruby with a stroll and a strut that usually caused a car to stop. One did and Ruby took the opportunity to cross the street.

Reaching the stoop, Ruby slowed enough to hoist the grocery bags and take the first of twelve steps to apartment 3D. Even on this sunny day the stairwell was dark, so Ruby found her keys as she walked the steps and cursed the shadowy walk space. The key slipped into the lock with a burdened familiarity and Ruby leaned into the opening door.

She closed the door with the same leaning motion that she had opened it with and let the grocery bags slide onto the floor. A relief or at least the sense of a coming relief grew in her. After checking the windows and closets and flipping on the bathroom light, she felt more comfortable. She kicked her shoes one, then the other, beneath the bed and hoped for their thud against the wall on the other side. Thud. Thump.

Ruby's breath calmed and she felt safe in her home.

After a moment on the bed she thought of making Harold's dinner. He would be almost home—maybe he was still on the school bus. She scurried to the kitchen with thoughts of his sixteen-year-old face. Thoughts of Harold brightened the dingy walls of the room.

Harold turned the knob and opened the door excitedly, "Mama?" She grinned at him from the kitchen. "Mama, did you forget that the big game is tonight? We playin' the Wild Cats over in West Jersey!" His purple and yellow letterman's jacket fell into a dinner table chair. "West Jersey?" Her excitement matched his own. "Just how you getting to West Jersey?" "Me and Carl are ridin' in Bud's car. After the game, we'll grab some burgers and sleep over at Leroy's," Harold told his mother.

"Now Harold, you know I don't fancy you running around everywhere. Any which way you turn horrible things happen." Ruby tried to sound more stern than the concern she felt growing from deep inside her.

"Yeah, I know, Mama, but tonight is special. It's what the school's been waitin' for for a long time. It's the big game, mama. I just gotta go!" Harold's voice tried to be pleading. He wanted to show her that he knew what she feared and that he had worked it over in his head. He wanted to show her how much tonight meant to him. Instead, he brooded.

Ruby frowned, but conceded, "Well, let's eat dinner and I'll think on it." Harold smiled, then kissed his mother on the cheek before heading to his room and a change of clothes. Ruby watched him walk away and thought how handsome her six-footer had become. She had worked and sacrificed to get him this far. If they could just hold on a little longer he might stay out of danger. She might just be able to get him out of this God-forsaken neighborhood. If he kept his grades up he would be eligible for the football scholarship, his coach had said. Penn State was looking at him.

After dinner, Harold helped to clear the table. He carried the plates and glasses into the kitchen and leaned them into the sink asking, "Hey, Mama, did you think on me going to the game, yet?"

Ruby scratched through her black, curly hair and settled her eyes on her only son. "Harold, you know I want you to do things with your friends and all. It's just so much happenin' these days. I've decided to let you go if you're back in this house by eleven o'clock tomorrow night. No later. Do you understand me?"

"Mama, you're the best mama on this earth! I'll make it back here on time!" Harold couldn't believe that his mother agreed to let him go to New Jersey, but he had already told his friends that he was going and they would be by the house soon. At that same moment, a car horn blew from the street. Harold looked out of the window then turned to his mother, "Boy, those guys are here already." Ruby couldn't help but to laugh at his mock surprise. Harold grabbed his purple and yellow jacket from the back of the kitchen chair, then a piece of pie from the stove and kissed his mother on the cheek. With a big, happy grin on his face he said to Ruby, "You know Mama, I really love you," then he was out the door.

"I love you, too," Ruby said back to her son with a forced smile on her face, then she started washing the dishes.

After the dishes Ruby could find nothing interesting on the television. By eight o'clock she decided to go on to bed. Exhausted from the day and from making the difficult decision to let Harold go away for the night, she fell asleep right away. She slept quite comfortably until around one o'clock, when she was awakened by a scuffling sound that seemed to be coming from the living room.

The apartment was dark when she sat up in bed to listen closer to the noise. It was still there, still coming from the living room. Ruby's worst fears all came flooding back to her and she fought hard to stay calm, to keep down her hysteria. She wished that she had left a lamp on, even though Harold wasn't coming home tonight. She thought of climbing under the bed and of hiding in the closet. She wanted to be anywhere but in this apartment, right now. Then, Ruby remembered the .38 in the night stand. She nervously eased open the drawer and slipped her fingers over the revolver that lay on the family Bible. Slowly, she slid one finger into the trigger eyelet and over the wooden handle and lifted the gun out of the drawer.

When she bought the gun, the salesman promised that it was reliable. "You need to protect yourself and your family," he had said. She had already been convinced. Then he had shown her how to use it, "Just point and squeeze." She watched him closely but had never actually practiced the motion herself. She had come home and showed the gun to Harold; told him where she would keep it; and kept it loaded.

Throwing the covers back, she raised herself to a sitting position in the bed. Then, as quietly as she could, she got up from the bed. The gun was heavy, so Ruby held it with both hands. Now it felt cold. She hated having to use this gun, tonight. She hated the gun and she hated the noise coming from the living room. Ruby trembled. She dared herself to take a step. She was trembling more now, but cautiously took small, tip-toeing steps toward the open door.

Ruby stretched her neck to look around the door frame. She had a clear view of the window and took a heavy breath when she saw the huge outline of a man climbing into her living room window. She tried not to scream, but thoughts and visions of the neighborhood flashed through her mind. The figure, the man, moved farther into the apartment. When his foot patted softly against the floor, Ruby screamed out uncontrollably. Her fright took over her actions and as she screamed she began firing the gun at the shadow moving into her home. She remembered the instructions. "Point. Now, squeeze-shoot!" and Ruby felt herself pulling the trigger. Once! Twice!

The figure of the man fell into the apartment and landed on the living room floor. Ruby was shaking, but remembered to call 911. She fumbled in the darkness until she reached the end table with the big lamp and a telephone. She felt the blood pumping hard in her chest. Fright and anticipation trembled her hand as she reached and turned on the lamp.

It was the yellow that first caught the light of the lamp, then the purple. The pistol in Ruby's hand grew heavier. She moved toward the body and the familiar colors of the jacket. The body, the intruder did not move. His long, lean body stretched over the floor beneath the window with a familiarity. It was the shape of his head; the length of his hair; it was the way that his fingers seemed to be beckoning. Ruby knew this man. She knew this man, well—too well.

The gun slipped from her hand and landed hard against the carpeted floor and Ruby felt the scream building in her chest. The intruder was Harold. The scream vomited from her throat.

Her neighbors were banging on the door when Ruby fell to the floor beside her son. His face was still warm and motionless. She touched it again and again. Harold did not move into her touch. He did not moan. Ruby hugged him. She craddled him near her, like when he was a boy; and she cried. Her tears fell onto him; covering his closed eyes, his cheek and neck. Ruby wanted him to say something, to wake up, but he could not feel the warmth of her tears. He could not feel the way that Ruby held him nearer to her and rocked him until his blood became a bond between them. He could not feel her, but Ruby rocked her only son, just like this, to the pounding of neighbors at the door and neighbors on the street below.

At first the sirens were faint, like pin pricks to Ruby's ears. Somewhere in the haze Ruby could feel them getting closer. She felt the pricks growing closer and more intense. She felt the long, hot stretches of sound permeate the air by degrees. Finally, the prickly-heated sirens were on top of Ruby. They landed suddenly upon her ears with a blunt force and urgent recognition.

Outside her door the pounding of Ruby's neighbors subsided and she could feel the sticky heat of running on the staircase. The prickly sirens had brought the paramedics and the police. The paramedics were coming now for her son. The police were coming for her intruder. The neighbors were coming for the sight of it all. Ruby had always thought that they would be coming for her in this neighborhood, on some long, dark night. Ruby thought that a gun would help delay their arrival. She thought that she could pull the trigger when the time came.

Ruby looked down at the long, muscular body of her only son and knew that her life's work was done. She had raised him to be a good boy and he repaid her by being too good on this night. She wished that he had stayed in New Jersey, like he said that he was going to do. Ruby felt the force of the door opening onto her apartment. She felt the heavy hallway light burning down against the side of her face. She knew that her neighbors would see her craddling Harold's dead body. She knew that they would see his life stamped out on the floor. She knew that if they looked just a little harder that they would see hers on that floor, as well.

VON

That's What My Ass Is For

I was on the bus one day, and there I was sitting in my usual spot behind the driver. I was writing something because the trips on the bus had given me so much to think about. Anyway, I heard these heavy footsteps, and I looked up. It was one of my sisters. In an effort to take it a little easier on my overweight sisters, I'll just say she was big. She sat down directly across from me, and she had this really small pocket-book-sized umbrella in her hand. No problem. It looked like rain. But I immediately wondered exactly what her big ass was going to accomplish with that itsy bitsy teenie weenie umbrella. For the next couple of stops I wondered what she was going to prevent from getting wet. Then as I followed a trail that started from the umbrella in her hand up to her face, it hit me. Her hair. It was her hair. She was going to sacrifice everything else for the sake of her hair. Now don't get me wrong. It was laid. Li-zaid. Fried. Dyed. And laid to the side. Had a few waves in the front. A few crimps in the back. Some gold highlights to set it off. I'm sure she had spent a pretty penny on that weave. So shit, I don't blame her for protecting her investment. But needless to say, the whole scene sparked something within me that forced me to contemplate this situation—me and my sisters and our collective dilemma with our hair. The things we've gone through. The drastic measures we've taken. And the grave sacrifices we have made to keep our "dos" done.

I have just recently gone through a small renaissance, a rebirth, with my hair. Earlier this year I woke up one day and said, "fuck it." I had managed to let my hair grow down my back, and my monthly "relaxer" was accompanied by endless compliments of how pretty my hair was. Somehow, in the course of our history here in this mass confusion called America, we've managed to support the opinion that long hair and pretty hair are one in the same. So now "long" and "pretty" fall under the same definition when it comes to hair. A lot of times my hair would look horrible. Just scraggly. My ends would need clipping. My scalp would need oiling. And it was just dry and flaky. Nevertheless, some sister would always grant me a much desired compliment and tell me my hair was pretty.

Well, one almost spring Monday morning in March I woke up (in more ways than one) and staggered over to the bathroom. I looked in the mirror in total disgust at this bird's nest that sat on top of my head. If there had been a pair of scissors on the bathroom counter, I swear I would have cut it myself—right then and there. I needed a perm . . . again. My hair was growing so fast that I was now giving myself a retouch about every three weeks. Either my new growth was returning much too quickly or my hair had become immune to the stuff I was using on it. I was much too tired of worrying about it every . . . single . . . day. So I grabbed my copy of Houston's "Black Pages" and prayed I could find a salon open on Mondays so that I could get a trained, licensed professional to get rid of this shit. No luck. But you best believe that Tuesday afternoon, I was sitting in somebody's salon chair, watching what was once my glory fall to the floor to be later swept up and dumped in the trash.

Meanwhile, other people actually came from the other side of the shop to witness this event as if it was some kind of grand, holy ceremony. You could have almost sworn that Jesus was coming . . .

"You gone cut off all that hair?"

"You ain't scared?"

"Why you cuttin' all yo hair off like that?"

"I wouldn't never cut my hair off if it was that long."

"Girl, I'm tryin' to let mines grow."

I was not happy that they were making a spectacle out of me, especially since I was a bit skeptical anyway. Not about my decision to whack it off, but I had reservations about letting some bitch cut my hair who I didn't know and who didn't know me. What if it wasn't cute when she finished? I was sure of one thing though. If she fucked up my hair, it was gonna be *on*. And I was personally going to see to it that this was the last head of hair she fucked up. I waited patiently as she wicked and whacked, clipped and curled, until finally . . . there I was.

Sleek and sassy. I couldn't wait for the next day to begin so that I could start my first full day with my fresh, new look. I felt as though a burden had been lifted. That the person inside of me should have cut her hair long ago. That I was much too jazzy, much too free-spirited to have had that bunk and boring long hair for so long. That everything about me had grown and evolved into a whole new level of consciousness— everything except my hair which seemed to have carried itself over from a period when I was a happy-go-lucky sorority girl, bopping around Louisiana cheating on my boyfriend. So there, I fixed it . . . or so I thought.

I still wasn't satisfied. I mean, I liked my hair. And it was quite funny to watch the different comical reactions it brought forth in friends I hadn't seen since my transformation. But I still longed for that bright and glorious morning when I would awaken to a day filled with hope and promise, yet free of curling irons and oil sheen. My outlook on life and my way of thinking were already far past complicated, so I wanted to embrace a hair style that added simplicity.

The more I thought about it, the more I realized the sacrifices we, as black women, have made for our hair over the course of our kinky existence. From Madam C. J. Walker and the straightening comb to Luster's Jheri Curl to Blue Magic Hair Grease to "Just For Me." We've tried it all, just to stake our claim in this world of "Goldie Locks" and "Repunzels," bidding us to let down our immaculate flowing tresses. I hear our younger ones who are barely able to read and write, already referring to hair as "good" or "bad." We gotta put a stop to this shit somewhere. What are our children to do once they realize that they resemble neither Cinderella nor Pocahontas? Who ever said that "good hair" meant long and blonde or dark and wavy? Well, if versatility is good, then we're on the top of the list. We can do anything to our hair. Fry it or dye it. Freeze it or tease it. Wave it or shave it. Curl it or twirl it. Braid it or fade it. And we ain't gotta wash it everyday to keep it clean. Sounds all "good" to me. Besides, my mama always said, "All hair is good if it ain't falling out."

I say we create our own nappy-headed sister hero to prevent our little girls from having to grow up with towels draped across their fore-heads, pretending to swing their long gorgeous hair behind their backs.

And no matter how many other women would like to join us in our struggle, "sistuhs" are alone in this one. We can't go swimming. We won't get caught dead in the rain. We can't just wake up and wash it in the morning and be through. We can't fuck in the shower. We gotta tie it up at night. We gotta pay somebody else to do it. So many simple joys sacrificed. All for a relaxer. No lye? No lie. And you know what else? My girlfriend in college whose mother works with the coroner said that the tops of our skulls are green from all those chemicals we use to get perms, or shall I say "permanents." Is there something so awful about the natural texture of my hair that I should desire to "perm" it, that is, permanently straighten it? And who am I to deny my hair the opportunity to grow in its natural form with its natural texture?

Suddenly, I wanted to remember what my real hair felt like. I thought back to the days in my mama's South Dallas kitchen. I remembered sitting scrunched up in that dining room chair, submissively yielding to the torture that Madam C. J. Walker started. I remembered the occasional breeze that blew in through the screen on the back door which was open to let the burnt hair smell out. I remembered how hard I cried each time because of my constant fear that she would burn me. I remembered how wonderfully proud I felt when I looked in the mirror after the tears had dried. But what I could not remember for the life of me was what my hair felt like before the silky transition. I wanted to feel me—the natural, unaltered, unprocessed, real me. The real me that grew so wildly out of my scalp, having been concealed from myself and everybody else for so long that I never even knew its existence. And upon grasping this new revelation, I stood up and learned the true meaning of new growth.

I don't want my hair "relaxing." I would much rather have it standing at attention—on duty, so to speak—armed and guarding that which rests up under my scalp . . . my brain. Protecting it from radiation, ultraviolet rays, extreme temperatures, holes in the ozone layer, and other uncontrollable forces. This is the true purpose of the kink. To protect our brain which makes us think. No other race on god's green earth can swear allegiance to the kink. It is uniquely ours. I have chosen to envelope it. So with the help of a pair of common house scissors and a very flexible, adjustable mirror, I fired every strand of my hair that was "relaxing," and retained the true warrior hair. Hair prepared to protect and defend. Hair that chose to get up and party instead of merely lying around the house all day.

Of course, I haven't forgotten my days of snap, crackle, and pop with the hot curlers. I still have the burn scar on my face as a constant reminder. But more importantly, I have forgotten about that brother who longs to run his fingers through my hair—it won't be none of that. I've been holding on to your nappy shit for all these years, so don't sweat me about mine. And if you need something to hold on to amidst our fierce, animalistic heat of passion, well . . . that's what my ass is for.

GREG JOHNSON

Notes of a Funeral Director

I LOVE TO SEE DEAD BLACK BOYS
DRESSED IN SUNDAY'S BEST
SOLEMN, NO RAGE, IN SILK-LINED SLUMBER
I LOVE TO SEE DEAD BLACK BOYS
LAUDED BY PASSIONATE MOTHERS
TEARY-EYED DADDYS AND GIRLFRIENDS
JUMPING, JUMPING TO MOURNER'S SILENT TUNES
I LOVE TO SEE DEAD BLACK BOYS
MASSAGED WITH WORDS NEVER FELT IN LIFE
ATTUNED NOW AND STRIKING A VULNERABLE POSE
I LOVE TO SEE DEAD BLACK BOYS
CLUTCHING THE BIBLE OR THEIR FAVORITE GATT
LOWERED INTO THE GROUND AS PRAYERS AND
FORTY OUNCES OF RAIN BID THEM FAREWELL
I LOVE TO SEE DEAD BLACK BOYS
TESTIMONIES TO WORKS UNFINISHED
EYES THAT CLOSED WITH FEW EXPECTATIONS
I LOVE TO SEE DEAD BLACK BOYS
BLACK DEAD BOYS
BOYS DEAD BLACK
DEAD BLACK BOYS

Mary Had a Big Booty &
JC Ate a Plate of Collard Greens

NEWS RELEASE: *Esoterica State Univ. Dept. of Classical Civiliza-tions has confirmed centuries-old allegations. Evidence has deter-mined that Mary, mother of Jesus Christ, had a voluptuous roll below the ninth vertebrae. And, secret Church manuscripts disclose that Jesus Christ ate the cooked leaves of the brassica nigra plant as his last meal.*

yeah, mary had a big-o-booty
juicy motor, nice and 'round
how else could she 'scape to egypt
without ever being found?

yeah, mary had a big-o-booty
all them paintings full ah flaws
raphael's po' sick messiah
ain't got nuff butt to hold his draws

jesus ate a plate ah collard greens
toward the closing of life's doors
on the cross he hung triumphant
hot sauce runnin' out his pores

jesus ate a plate ah collard greens
at the dinnah 'fore he died
just sat talking to his brothers
looked into their eyes with pride

jesus ate a plate ah collard greens
and the scientists grew sicker
found when Romans pierced his skin
that out came blood and warm pot-liquor . . .

BERTRAM BARNES

She Hates Me

she hates me I can feel it under my skin

she is a dark woman
who waits in the shadows
of evening with lips
as juicy and pink as pomegranate

her eyes roll in her head
is she insane or just
tired of trifling niggers

joy must not be in some remote by-an-by
it must be in the sweetness of the moment
in which I am living
I tell the whole damn world that
point blank

she folds her arms and sighs
she smiles
her madness is diminishing
her fears entering the zone of rationalization

she hates me I can smell it
I don't want to know her name
but her lips are heavy and voluptuous
like those I saw on the dancing goddess
in bourbon street: that hell hole
the french quarter

I would like to dance
with the wild goddess of night
and fear orgies

maybe this is she
the androgynous shiva, a black diva
in the body of a university girl

she shifts her books
her breasts are as large and full
as 40 ounce bottles of beer

I would like to get high on her
drink her dry
maybe if I called out to her
sweet and low
like a calf
to a milk cow
she would let me suck them

I think it's mother nature
out to self actualize
to get herself an education
to become a captain of industry

how many times have I prayed
to meet again the mayan
who swam naked in the river
when I was a little hoodlum
in arkansas

if she weren't nature
what is
if to be natural isn't the ultimate end of education
what is

maybe this is she
how divinely beautiful she was
with a vagina as lively and slippery as a rainbow trout

if she would dance with me
I would ask her to marry
then sleep with her
and cut holes in the condoms

she would wake up with
a black minnow swimming
up the narrow river to her soul
flipping and flapping in the fallopian tubes

nine months after she would bear me a son
and I would teach him to sing off key
to dream subversive dreams
to wear tattoos to manipulate the vote
to make math his slave, his con, his bitch, his religion
an eye=an eye
a tooth=a tooth

Doubt, question, confront, defy, create, produce, manage, protect
Never take your eye balls off the bottom line, son
Meditate, concentrate, incorporate, conquer
Barricade the entry, monopolize, patent
Restrict the supply and raise the price,
Squeeze the competition's nuts in a vice

i'd tell him about the importance of
philanthropy and endangered species
pathos, ethos, chaos, oceans and thermonuclear power
i'd speak of the ancient egyptians, greeks, romans, chinese, inca,
nubians
                and the myths of the yoruba, eskimos, choctaws and germans

i'd insist he wear his hair like the rastas
as long as he slept under my roof and ate my tofu
and when his mother
the dark stranger complained
of my trifling ways and miseducation

I would soothe her with sweet words and turquoise earrings
i'd kiss her breasts and salivate her soul into
tortured orgasms
i'd make her believe that she was the queen of spades
and I was the king
i'd give her sports cars, money, houses, land, affection, time, credit
cards, race horses, space,
respect, sensitivity, tenderness
i'd part her thighs
and plant an oak tree there

and the acorns would become
so many thousands of little giggling girls
with green leaves for hair
and I would say now teach them self reliance, womanist criticism,
post colonial criticism
and to stop that damn giggling
and everything else you want them to know
we rasta will dance to yall's music
we'll cook the corn meal porridge
we'll wash and iron the clothes
and we'll mop this nasty floor

and after i'd gotten them all drunk
and blind with power
i'd take those acorn headed children
and that grasping rasta
and that red-lipped, heavy hipped fool
and fling them over the edges

of the earth and into lakes
and oceans and clouds and comets and stars

I would make them drink sweat and eat sorrow
I would lay my hands on them
I would make them as immortal as the milky way

she hates me I can taste it

CASSANDRA M. BAILEY

Natural Beauty

You don't see me (during the
summer) running out to get a tan.

                You don't see me wearing a
                lip liner to enlarge thin lips.

      You don't see me wearing alot of make-
      up, in order to add color to my face.

                    I am almond,
                    butterscotch,
                    caramel,
                    chocolate,
                    chocolate-chip,
                    fudge.

        I have small,
        medium,
        large,
        beautiful,
        luscious,
        kissable,
        full
              lips.

I need no additives and no substractives.

                I am a Natural Beautiful
                Black Woman, inside and out
                (whether you see it or not).

                I am perfect just the way I am . . .
                In my natural beauty.

ANTHONY A. DOUGLAS

Thanks, But No Thanks

While in a big burnt sadness
looking like a whole bunch of hugs
that never happened
you walk up unwanted
having a perfectly politically correct day
and I try to leave but instead I say
I never liked your happy-ass any way
because I overflowed that little pot
and got me a great big pity tub
with a sorrow pad and I'm about to scrub
all the gleam out your eyes
giving your joyful ass
a cascade of long hard cries
over goodtimes you've had
and goodtimes I've missed
ducking bullets, 40 ounce bottles
and all kinds of other SH it

So if you really want to help then please
do this one small thing, if not for yourself, then for me
take all your guilty-assed feelings
and all those little helpful social perks
and find you some new minority to suck-up to
or even better yet
SIT
YOUR POLITICALLY-CORRECT-ASS DOWN
somewhere else
and shut the fuck up!

CHUCK PERKINS

Jazz Funeral

the very soft
slow
euphonic rhythm of the jazz band
ripens the atmosphere
a myriad of screams
shouts
and tears
seem to blend in with the solemn moment
almost as if the horns and drums
had a melodious cry of their own

with a forty ounce in one hand
and a cigarette in the other
to calm my nerves
and soothe my soul
along with the others
I gently rock from side to side
as the young brother's casket
is brought from the sanctuary of the church
to the back of a hearse
where we all began to prepare
for his last dance
his last ride
his last party

the African sisters who nurtured this man-child
are having fits
'cause at seventeen

you can't help but think of what he could have been
but today
he's just dead
another young
misguided
misdirected warrior
whose life has been sucked from within his breast
permanently
forever
for nothing

as we move away from the church
the euphonic rhythm has changed
it is no longer soft and sad
it is now wild
happy
and is a sense
a little mad
when you throw your hands in the air
and gracefully
and emphatically
move your body in a way that only Africans can
an unpatterned way
that's natural to you
and flows with the music
down in New Orleans
we call that the *second line*

our body's language says to this young brother
that this dance is for you
yes, this last dance is for you
we dance   that your last vision of us can be a happy one
as we party past the housing projects
this is the last time to see your playground
and battle field
this vicious

brutal
familiar enclave of blackness
where you endured much pain and hurt
mingled with laughter and love
this is the last time to see
 the rough
happy
innocent
nappy headed little boys on their bikes
that reminds you so much of yourself
when you were ten and innocent
the last time to see
the old sisters sitting on the porches
becoming wiser by the day
and the old brothers
sitting in front of the liquor stores
reminiscing about what could have been
this is the last time to see your life and your world
because of that
we stomp today
we cry today
we dance today
yes we dance today
when we get to the candy store
the place where your life was quickly halted
the euphonic rhythm changes yet again
this time the music and the people are in a frenzy
they danced like this will be the last time
before we all get to see our maker
and as the music pounds
and thumps
and blares
and draws us all into this intense moment
twelve of your best hommies remove your casket from the hearse
in a way equivalent to the white boys hip-hip hooray
your boys thrust your casket to the sky

and they take it down
and they thrust it again
triumphantly
angrily
repeatedly
as if to say to your assassin
muthafucker
you can't touch him now
not your guns
not your bullets
can't touch him now
however
in the midst of this frenzy
the roaring sound of a hot vicious bullet rips through the air
perhaps
this is the assassin's rebuttal
this bullet must sound like the fat lady
cause the party is over
African brothers sisters babies seek refuge
desperately trying to avoid their last dance
but deep down inside
we all know
that we will dance again
again soon

KEITH WALKER

My Blackness

Sometimes I let my pants hang down
And make wrinkles around my shoes
Sometimes I play rap music real loud
While I'm driving around my school
Sometimes I go into a quiet restaurant
And just trip and act a fool
Sometimes I show my blackness off
Like a rare and precious jewel

I stopped gang-banging and selling drugs
And letting stereotypes be my guide
I still feel the black man's aggression
But I try to keep it held inside
I roll down my window to let my black skin show
When I'm cruisin' in my ride
I sport my blackness like an Italian suit
Because I've always had black pride

Sometimes, on purpose, I'll talk aloud
At a movie I'd gone to see
And I'll already have a grin prepared
For when you turn to stare at me
So I don't flinch when you call me a thug
'Cause I'm cool with my identity
I show my blackness in everything I do
And I'll never forget my streets

Do you get upset when I make A's in school
And I laugh up and down the halls
Do you find it offensive when I let my pants hang low
And show off half my draws
Do you think it's prejudice when I greet every black
And walk by you without a pause
I show my blackness in everything I do
My work, my poetry, my all

MICHAEL OLLIE CLAYTON

The Mask

Travis is convinced that
there is a certain way to
hold a cigarette,
and most certainly
that there is a particular way
to pull on it: Gangsta, gangsta
the nicotine's still the same.
Travis also believes there's
a certain way to talk
only one way to walk
—so did his buddy, Calvin,
whose body, last night
was outlined in chalk.
Travis thinks there's only
one neighborhood: His!
And I hope this man-child
with the wavy hair, cat eyes,
smile of a star, full crotch
and the body of a warrior
lives long enough for the kids
coming up behind him
to show him a new walk
and a new talk
—maybe they can pull the mask
off his face.

GAYLE BELL

Ain't I Got an Issue
(Borrowed from Harriet Tubman's "Ain't I a Woman")

Inevitably, it never fails;
I'm in your house, or
we're organizing for "our common cause"
Anyway I'm in your face and you need to vent
you catch me off guard with a statement (tho well meant)
that I have to call you on
and instead of you *hearing* what I'm *saying*
you say "Hey, I have an issue"
and it could be any issue
pick one
food addition issue
class issue
color issue
etc . . . issue
but, of course, you're working on
your healing
so I shouldn't take myself so
personally
so in answer to that
I gotta ask you
AIN'T I GOT AN ISSUE!
honey, I have enough agendas
to keep all the talk shows happy
but you can't relate
I shouldn't take it that way
well; just cause therapy for black sistas
wasn't something we talked about over coffee
. . . and the only time we sat on anyone's couch
was cause we were forced to

being interpreted by a Euro-drug addicted and god knows what else
fraud
who wouldn't have recognized with a Rorschach
doesn't mean I can't relate to you
What this you say!
I must ed-u-cate you!
honey, why do u think there's a u in the word
for decades we have had
your culture and traditions
jettisoned down our throats
so handy for those SAT's
and immigration citizenship
that we require to gain a toe hold in
your melted pot
and just because you have
taken a women's studies class
featuring Audre, bell, and Angela
doesn't mean you know who I am
and the herstory of my sista's multiculture
AIN'T I GOT AN ISSUE
just because I'm sitting in a co-chair next to you
doesn't mean I have to sign all my other sister up
for a seat at your table
Ain't I got an issue
when your inclusiveness leaves us out
gives a no voice
ain't I got an issue
when I HAVE to take you to task and ask that you
OWN YOUR SHIT!
and you tell me I'm being overly sensitive
and thin skinned
So in closing my sisters
learning about my path
requires steps taken in MY direction
because if I have to be the bridge
to my back

All I get
is walked on
AND THIS BRIDGE IS SHAKY

OLD BLACK MEN

CLUB MANS TALC

BRUSHED LIBERALLY ON A FRESHLY SHAVED NECK

DUTCH MASTERS SMOKED TO THE NUB

AND CHEWED WITH SIGNIFYING PRECISION

HOLDING COURT OVER MY MUCH TOO LOUD UNCLES

AND ON HOLIDAYS

THE WHISKY/ROCK CANDY CORDIAL BREATH

I MISS THE SMELL OF OLD BLACK MEN

THE GLOW OF BLUING

ON A HEAVILY STARCHED WHITE SHIRT

AND LARGE CALLOUSED HARD WORKING HANDS

HANDS THAT SCOOP ME UP AND SWING ME ROUND

AND UP TOWARD HEAVEN

I MISS THE FEEL OF OLD BLACK MEN

THE SAME HANDS THAT WRUNG THE NECKS OF CHICKENS

AND DRESSED AND SMOKED THE HOGS

AND SOMETIMES

THE SAME HANDS THAT WOULD PUT A SMILE

ON OLD AUNT BERTA'S FACE

WALKING STOOP TALL FROM THE LIFE LABORS

BUT GETTING TICKLED AT IT ALL

JUST TO SPITE FATE TO ITS FACE

I MISS THE SOUND OF OLD BLACK MEN

THE WAY OF OLD

BLACK MEN

MICHELE L. MAJORS

Downtown Brothers

I want to see a brother
with a toothpick in his mouth
Give me tall
Short
Dark
Light
Yellow
Black
Blue Black
Chocolate kiss
Sexy
Leaning
High top fades
College cuts
Smooth, chic bald
like Michael Jordan

I want him walking with his suit and tie on
Swaying to the downtown groove
I want him with his hard hat on and utility belt swinging
from his fine—umph

Can't find a downtown brother in the suburbs
Gotta find him working
Chilling
In downtown

I want to see him holding a building up
I want to see him swirl that toothpick

Roll it and taste it
Like he would me

I want to pull back
Dark shades and see
Sexy
Downtown brother's Brown eyes staring at me

Even my sweet brothers look good
Even though they don't want someone like me

I want a downtown brother
You know what I'm talking about

The ones you see walking

Excuse me
Strutting
Chest out
The ones that fill your head
Make you have wicked thoughts in elevators Ooh
Give me a downtown brother
Any day

MONICA FRAZIER

I Ain't Mad At'Cha

Me and daddy was in the bed chilling
Like we like to do
When we watch the news.
They did a long story on black mens.
Called it "Threatened With Extinction"
Said brothers was missing that knowledge
In College
And getting their wisdom
In prison.
Then they talked about hopeless black babies
Musta been born of ghetto virgins,
Cause they ain't got no visible daddies.
On and on they went.
Colors and crack.
All stuff like that.
By then, our chill was cold.
Daddy turned it off.
I looked at him hard
And I said,
"Baby, you ever been to jail?"
"Nope," he said.
So I asked him,
"Baby, you ever robbed anybody?"
"Nope, cain't say I have," he replied.
"Well, baby, surely you done shot somebody.
What kind of black man is
                you if you ain't shot nobody?"
"I hit a bird with a bb gun once."

"Man, that don't count."

"Oh," he said.

"What you doing here anyway? All married and being a good daddy to your children."

(We laughed)

Which reminds me

"Baby, can you take the kids to school tomorrow?

I want to sleep late."

"Sure," he said.

Then we both said,

"I love you. Goodnight."

ZENAURA MELYNIA SMITH

Soul Soother

I'm light as a feather
Heavy as a stone
And soft as new snow in the winter
I'm a cup of hot cocoa on a cold icy day
I'm the rain in fall
I'm the comforter
The soother
It's my shoulder that you cry on
I'm the peacemaker
I settle the soul
I wipe away your problems
With the waving of my hand
As I settle you to sleep
I summon the crickets to sing you a tune
For they are my orchestra
The night is my body
The moon is my smile
And quieting your soul is my specialty

FRED FOWLER

Tribute to Watermelon

Watermelon so delectable and sweet
the color of our pride
watermelon be the red meat
watermelon be the black seeds
watermelon be the green rin'
with nectar from mother earth's finest vine
watermelon is the fruit of thought
watermelon is a history taught hand-to-mouth
north—east—west—south
watermelon is simple, soul pleasures recalled
when we were just plain black folks
sticky fingers and all!

FREDDI WILLIAMS EVANS

Ms. Hanah's Hair

Ms. Hanah's hair tells a story
A silent story
Full of tears and glory
A story, ninety years in the making

Her resilient curls
All tight and twisted
Echo how they RESISTED, Resisted, resisted
What society insisted
      hot combs, lye and straightening aids
      grease, gels and pomades
      all promising to change
      what nature made.

Her bushy style
So bold and beautiful
Whispers jokes and ridicule
'Bout bad hair that was hard to rule
      it was picked, pulled, plaited and permed
      while Hanah sat for hours and dared not squirm.

Her fine strands
Now white like snow
Cry stories of stress, strain and struggles
That only Hanah would know
      stories of ups and tales of down
      telling how she earned her cottony-soft crown.

Hanah's hair shouts VICTORY!
Honor and Glory.
Her hair is a testimony
It is her story
> Don't need mousse nor spray
> It stands on its own

Ancient . . . Affirming . . . Natural

VICKY CHARLESTON

if I should die tonight

if I should die tonight
I want someone to
go into my bathroom and
kill that fly that's been
buzzing around my light all week
i've been tryin' to kill that thing
for days now, it was just too quick
for me, but if i'm gonna die
I want it dead too . . .
so somebody kill it for me.

my insurance papers are
in a brown envelope
in the third drawer of
my dresser in the washroom,
I put 'em there right next to that
.38 special my daddy gave me,
he knew I didn't like guns
but said he would feel better
if I had one around,
he rigged that thing to sound
like a cannon when it goes off,
he said a sound like that would
scare anybody away,
so I wouldn't have to worry
too much about my aim,
besides, he said, I needed
some kind of home security,

if I wasn't gonna have a big dog
or a big man around,
it'd be best if I had a big gun,
that's where my insurance papers are,
in that third drawer next to that
big gun . . . safe and secure.

if I should die tonight,
don't bury me in anybody's ground,
I want to be burned, burned to a crisp
get my brown boots,
I should have thrown those things out
long ago, but no matter how worn out
they became, I always felt right
when I had 'em on,
the soles of those things could
probably tell you more about me
than I could . . .
if I should die tonight
don't throw them out . . .
burn those suckers with me,
then dump my ashes
in the deserts of new mexico
I always wanted to live there.

i'd like somebody to find
my frantic friend,
the one I tumbled around with
only a few short weeks ago,
the one who said he knew
what I needed,
the one who said he could give me
what I needed
if I should die tonight somebody
find him for me and tell him . . .
he was right . . .

tell him when I said I didn't
want to see him anymore that
I was really saying I was scared,
there's a statue of a man I made
with telephone wire that sits
on top of my t.v.,
if I should die tonight
take that wire man and
give it to him,
he'll know what it means . . ,
but make sure you let him know
I said he was one of the coolest guys
I ever met,
I was just scared that's all!

if I should die tonight
I want my sister to take my son,
he loves her, almost as much
as he loves me, he once said
and I know she loves him . . .
I can't imagine him being
anywhere else, not even
with his dad . . .
if I should die tonight
that's where I want him to go,
that's where I want him to stay,
where he'll be happy.

gather up all my poetry,
it's scattered here and there
in the dusty corners of my house
between stacks of newspapers, old
magazines, various junk drawers
and computer disks.
gather them all up, wrap them
in a plastic bag, stuff them

in my cedar chest and
give them to my son,
at nine, I think he's too young
to really know who I am,
I bet you right now all
he could tell you about me is:
I write too much, I talk too much,
I sing too much, I make a great
lasagne, the best fried chicken
in the whole world and
he'd prefer I not shake
that tambourine around the table
in the morning when he's trying
to eat his oatmeal . . .
I know you say you hate
that stuff son but
if I should die tonight . . .
you'd miss it . . .
and when you find yourself wishing
I hadn't left you so soon,
when you find yourself wishing
you could just talk to me,
just pull out that old cedar chest,
open up that plastic bag and dig in,
if I should die tonight son
I just wanted to let you know
you'll always be able
to find me there just waiting
to share a few words with you . . .
but first, make sure you get somebody
to kill that friggin' fly!

MONICA DENISE SPEARS

(untitled)

I'm
  not
     your
Mercedes
     450
      SEL
where
     you can rub
your
  car sanding
  cabbage shredding
  permanently ashy
hands
     over my
smooth and curvaceous
body

I'm
  not
     your
Bent
   ly
where
     you can relax
your
    tight-check
    spark flying
    penny pinching

ass
    in my
contour fitting
      sink
          in
             me
interior
and
ride
    me
till you get tired

If
you are having trouble following this
you
  clutch popping
  restricted license
  never had   never will
brother

I
  am
    not
      yours

Well Your Honor, this is how I remember things happening:

I had called the police on him before because that fool had been coming around causing trouble. He had been causing me two months of trouble. You know, knocking on my door all hours of the night; calling me on my job, shit, oh, I mean stuff, like that.

Well, one night, the man was just full of trouble and liquor. He busted through my door and messed up my house—turning over the chairs and knocking stuff off the t.v. He storms in my bedroom, grabbing me and then he started hitting on me. I was able to get away to call the police to come and get this crazy nigger before he had killed me. Well, he leaves just before the cops come. And when they get there, they come with this here at-tit-tude like I'm causing all the trouble by myself. See, like I was putting all of these here marks on myself.

So when they finally get around to asking me what happen, I tells them, "Look, I don't want no more trouble. I just want him gone away from me and I don't want him coming 'round me no more!" And then the black officer ask me who the man is and I tells him he my husband but we separated. Then the white officer say, "Well, have you thought about gittin' a restraining order or maybe you should put him on a peace bond." A peace bond!? Your Honor, that man wouldn't know peace unless it was wearing a mini-skirt and could touch her toes without bending her knees! So I says, "Okay, fine, but can't ya'll at least arrest the sonofabitch until I can go get one of those bonds and restraining orders?" Then, guess what they tell me Your Honor? "No." No?!! They says they couldn't arrest him because they didn't *see* him kick my ass. I just broke down and cried. Then they says, "We'll make a report ma'am, and it'll be on files, but this here is just another one of those domestic fighting cases." I'm saying to mysef, this nigga bust thru my door, grab me by my collar, throw me 'round the room, blacken my eye, and this here is just *another* domestic fight?! Shee', wasn't no fight—I ain't throwed no punches. Anyways, I say, "The only way ya'll can arrest him is if ya'll see him hit me?" And they says, "Yes!" I tries to explain every time this here happens, I loses a dayawork. I got four kids and two of them his. I can't afford to lose no money like that. So one week later, I go to get a restraining order.

Well, one week after I get the restraining order here he comes again—S.O.S! Oh, s.o.s.: Same ole shit—banging on the doors and windows, yelling my name. I calls the police and reports that this man is back and he ain't suppose to be around me. I told them to "Come and get this crazy black man or somebody's leaving ina motherfuckin' bodybag!" No disrespect to Your Honor, but I had had too much of this kinda action. Hitting on me, kicking me. Hell, felt like he was trying to kill me! So, after he bust thru the door he traps me in the kitchen. After he hits me the third time—at least I think it was the third time, I landed on the kitchen floor near the counter. And when I was trying to get up my hand touched the knife I was using for to cut up some onion. Before I'd known it, I had grabbed the knife and had stabbed him. And then he fell, grabbing his chest, crying an' shit. It's right about that time that the police come. I still had the knife in my hand and they arrest me—even though they didn't see me kill him.

saddi khali

she is running now . . .
what when she is dead

1.
with wind whippin her thots at breakneck speeds
she is running

she is running
trackstar hurdling the truth
there is no finish line

she is running
long-jump champion
vaulting her wall of pain
no records have been broken

she is running
thru ashes

asphyxiation.

wild horses cannot breathe
with dust flying in their nostrils
with madmen & lassos gripping the air like asthma

she runs
like a blind cheetah
chasing the sound of food

like cheap stockings

like the noses
of sick babies

if you love her
help her
if you care for her
help her slow down
to face the truth
stop to breathe

corner her
cover all exits
set up roadblocks in the street
don't let her get away from herself
you will know her if she passes

look for the eyes holding rain
like summer clouds

follow the trail of cocaine lines
dead children
empty liquor bottles
& her own skin/her blood

dying antelope running toward the vultures
willing prey/willing prey
let us all pray
ask god for assistance . . .
ask the spirits . . .
ask the ancestors . . .
ask mothers . . .
ask fathers . . .

asphyxiation.

life is running
trackstar/long-jump champion
wild horse/blind cheetah
dying antelope
running/jumping
running/jumping
running/jumping

& if somebody doesn't do something
fast . . .

she will run
all the way to the edge of herself

& jump.

2.
& what then
I mean she is dead
& gone

when her pain is no longer
an angry inmate slashing our faces
making wounds of our mouths
that we bleed concern/words
she cannot or refuses
to hear

what when she is dead

when air ceases to enter
& spread
what will we breathe then

when her need
is not here to make us men
when her smile
doesn't burst into powder
& soften our skin
but becomes broken bone
& dust
littering streets instead

what when she is dead
when her running has reached its end

the greatest horror & hope of it all
is . . .
as soon as she goes
another her will come

& what then . . .

FROSWA' BOOKER-DREW

Fantasy

He walks in
Smiles
Wide lips
Large hands
Brown, coffee coated complexion
Malcolm glosses
Facial hair
Umm.
"Ready," he offers
Reaching for my hands
Embracing them within his
Pulling me closer
Until my body joins his dance
Until his body comes snug against mine
I find the plateaus of his pleasure:
Lips on mine
Licking   Loving Losing everything
In his embrace
Time is not an issue of this essence
Light slips into darkness
And I am caught in that whirlwind
No need for restraint
"I need you," he confesses
And I respond with my body
And he understands the reply
I'm holding on
Watching the eclipse
Listening to the Richter register this quake

Spotting Haley's Comet
Saying goodbye to a Black family being picked up by a UFO
Phenomena
Phenomenon in our bodies
Phenomenal
And then, "Yes!"
Then,
The door bell finally rings

FREDDI WILLIAMS EVANS

Fly By

We got balloons at
Janell's birthday party.
All of my friends were there.
All, that is,
Except Rashan.

He was killed in a drive-by shooting
And everyone cried and cried.
Rashan like birthday parties
And
Big, round balloons, so,

I let my balloon go
Way up in the sky.
"Dear God, it's for Rashan," I yell.
"I want to tell him, HI!"

MAWIYAH KAI EL-JAMAN BOMANI

New Growth

always
in a room
full of spectators
my stepfather
sarcastically banters
"your hair
looks like
rolled up
mice titties
just like them
wild
shaka zulu
africans
on the news"
I smile
sometimes laugh
at just how funny
an 80 year old
jheri-curl wearing man
religiously worshipping
white people's hair
can be
trying desperately
to permanently
fry
dye

and lay to the side
that part of him
that won't let him forget
you can never
tame
your roots

ADRIENNE NORRIS

Dreams Befitting

The sky, a blanket of prickly dampness, competed with the shrill of pneumatic drills and off-colored remarks to make the August morning unbearable. The three men in hard hats and denim work clothes didn't say anything directly to the woman in the gray suit with the over-sized leather portfolio. But they watched her as she minced around puddles of gravel and then skittered across the street to the sawed off looking building on the town square.

"Who'd have thought," said one. "Some culture in this raggedy town."

"Yeah, and not bad looking, either."

Chelsea Franklin muscled open the door of the Portsville Art Center, which was stubborn with the stickiness of a Texas summer, and slipped inside.

With one hand she clutched her case and with the other she tried to smooth the copper tendrils that had escaped her French Roll and were beginning to frizz around her jaw line. As she dabbed at the perspiration cupping her cheeks, she forced herself not to peep through the glass doors like a child waiting for a spanking. She knew she was late. A row of patrons, their backs ramrod straight, their eyes trained on the empty podium, were in front of her. She felt coldness as she passed them, walking down the lonely center aisle, with only her echoing high heels for company. But she refused to be cowed, and she strode to the dais, pulled out her speech and lifted her chin.

From the corner of her eye, she saw her boss. Arthur Grahame, who was a big man, retreating into his office, back first. She lifted an eyebrow. Was he trying to warn her? Before her, the audience, middle aged and staid, seemed harmless. As she arranged her papers, she whispered, "It can't be that bad."

She was wrong.

"Look, Mama," a surprisingly young voice squeaked from a center row, "she's got a chocolate face."

Beneath the hushes that filled the silence, the woman froze. Chelsea Franklin, svelte, charming, with all the sophistication that she could buy in two years of travel through Europe, said not a word. She stood stunned, like a wounded animal, shot down by the precociousness of a five year old.

"They'll never listen to me now," she thought. Self pity iced through her, as sweat trickled down her back. The cold moisture pooled at the waistband of her skirt.

"She must be very, very bad, Mama. Her hands are dirty."

The eyes of the patrons, which had been glassy with a wry smugness, slid to the corners of the room.

"So, what," she thought. "I need this job." Chelsea knew that if she were to keep her position as the director of the choral group, Melange, she would have to get this group of button down benefactors to loosen its purse strings. She swallowed the lump in her throat. That would take eloquence, and the speech that she had pored over for hours would not do the job.

On top of that, her feet were killing her. That morning she had crammed them into three and a half inch suede shoes, thinking that they looked good with her suit, and now she was paying for it. Wildly, she looked around the room for anything that would distract from the throbbing pain, and give her inspiration for her speech. Nothing. It was absolutely hopeless.

The room, with its cement floors, dun colored walls and high, grimy windows, looked like an airplane hangar. Chelsea recalled that earlier she had tried to get her boss to set up a wine and cheese table for the patrons. But all the no nonsense Mr. Grahame had come up with for refreshments was a hastily covered card table holding day old doughnuts, a second hand coffee pot and a stack of styrofoam cups. "We're strapped," was his reply to her vacant look.

Chairs scraped under the weight of restlessness and Chelsea knew that she would have to do something drastic. Ignoring the papers on the podium, she turned to the audience.

"Good morning, Ladies and Gentlemen. On behalf of the Association for the Performing Arts, I would like to welcome you. As we all know, the arts: music, dance, theater, is a vital part of our heritage. And as you are also probably aware, funds in our own community of Portsville are being cut. Still, if we are to provide for our future and for the future of our children, we must continue our proud tradition."

She paused. Her words had not melted the glazed looks. She would have to try something else.

"I am happy to present to you, the distinguished choral group, Melange. These young people, from all parts of the Portsville community, will be performing for you later in the program."

Chelsea gave a flourish to the twenty or so teens who had bunched in a knot on the far side of the room. They stood as near to the door and as far away from the audience as possible. Chelsea moved the papers on the podium over a fraction of an inch. Maybe she had made a mistake. With their faces in shadow and shoulders hunched over, Melange presented a picture that was all too familiar in the minds of many—the rude, irresponsible teenager. She cleared her throat, trying to get the attention of her protege, Guillermo. But he, blind to the tension in the room, was sparring with his pal, Tony. The woman watched helplessly as her troupe muttered, shambled, and stole looks at the implaccable patrons. They, for their part, stared straight ahead, wanting to have as a little to do with the frightening youth as possible.

There was nothing left for her to do but barrel ahead.

"As I was saying, the arts, like many other interests in our city, needs . . . ."

A ball of mischief catapulted on the stage. She turned aside to see the little boy stand beside the dais, his pansy blue eyes staring up at her from under a shock of stawberry blonde hair. He reached up and tugged the sleeve of her silk jacket, and with pudgy fingers rubbed her arm.

"Mama, it doesn't come off."

Chelsea held her breath. This was really too much. Gripping the edges of the podium, she kept herself from reeling as a thin, blonde woman flashed in front of her. The wispy woman bent down and scooped up her son and carried him off in a flurry of embarrassment. "Sorry, sorry," tumbled over her shoulder like stones rolling down a hill. Chelsea did not have to look at the woman to know that when she got back to her seat, she strapped the boy in an arm hold, and she was not mollified when the mother stuck a toy in the kid's hand to keep him quiet.

Mortification roiled around Chelsea, dissolving her confidence. She felt as naked as she had on the day she had been handed over to the detox unit in the out-of-the-way hospital in upstate New York. She had hated that place. The odor of sanctification gagged her, even more than the stench of her own anger and self disgust. Even today, as she closed her eyes, she could see the smirks of the attendants as they snickered over the medical chart of the junkie who used to be a big Broadway star. That experience had been a waking nightmare. But she had battled back, and with the help of her boss, she had landed this job.

Her eyes riveted on the windows that reminded her so much of her cell in the hospital. Mr. Grahame couldn't help her now. She had messed up big time. She could forget about the funds for the art campaign. She could forget about the money for Melange. She could even forget about her job.

She sniffled, surprising herself at the childish habit. Her mother had been right. She, Chelsea Franklin, was selfish and would never be any good to anybody. The drug addiction had proved that. This fiasco, today, proved it, too.

The thirty-year-old African-American woman standing behind the podium, poised, lovely, articulate, was totally unable to distinguish anything around her. She couldn't feel the feet that had throbbed minutes earlier. She couldn't make out the words that puffed out of the faces wavering in front of her.

But she felt the anger. She knew it as something familiar that swirled around her until it sucked her into a vortex of ugliness. She slid downward until she fell into the deep, aching place.

She was a teenager again, sitting in a kitchen smothered with the smells of salt pork and collard greens boiling in an old scarred pot on a rickety stove. Over her, two women, the most important people in her life, hurled words at each other, choking out the last bit of peace in the cramped room.

Her mother rocked with righteousness and waggled a finger. In a voice bitter with sarcasm, she spewed, "This little miss needs to get her head out of the clouds. Might be she could even get a real job and help out around here." Her grandmother, a tiny woman, reared back and railed at the daughter who towered over her, "You leave that baby alone. She's got dreams. The good Lord will take care of her."

Then a look passed over her mother's face, a hurt, like when a child gets slapped for doing nothing at all, and Chelsea wondered for the thousandth time if the angry words had anything to do with her.

"He's only a little boy."

The mother's words gouged her from the audience, making her flinch, bringing her back into the moment, up from that low, aching place. Melange, seeing their teacher's pain, murmured in resentment.

"You ought to take that 'little boy' home and teach him some manners."

Tina, the outspoken member of the troupe, bobbed on her heels. Her outburst got nods of approval and rounds of "You got it, girl."

"Now just a doggone minute."

The boy's father stood up, knocking over his chair. Blue eyes blazed out of a face mottled with rage. People wrenched around, anxious to get a look at the man who stood well over six feet and who had a voice that scorned apologies.

"I won't let you or anyone else tell me how to raise my kid."

The males in Melange, one body, swung around and took a step toward him.

"Maybe we better go, dear." A woman in her late fifties, wearing a red cloth hat and matching cape, cast a worried look at the man who sat beside her. She bent over to pick up her purse, and her husband moved forward in his seat to help her, anxious to leave before the big fight.

His words blasted everyone in the room.

"My wife and I came to see the progam, and we're not budging."

Without a backward glance, he waved his arm toward Melange.

"You people think you got all the rights and can call the shots whenever you want." He folded his arms across his chest.

"Well, that's not happening here, not today."

He sat back down in his chair, and looked around to make sure that everyone knew that his family was staying put. The older couple stared at the floor, uncomfortable.

Chelsea darted a look at her boss, hoping that he had seen the spectacle and would jump in before the whole program turned into a brawl. But Arthur Grahame stood inside the door in silence, hands jammed in his pockets, a wave of dark hair covering his emotions. After long minutes, he sauntered over to the table with the forgotten refreshments, hunkered down to jab a plug into the outlet, and smiled.

Chelsea saw that grin, and standing in the middle of the feud, she let her mouth drop open in disbelief.

The anger from both sides had cooled and hardened, like a brick wall. She gathered her papers, ready to walk away for good, when she heard a scritch, scritching sound. Her eyes grazed the cement floor, and she saw a red yoyo zip around chair legs and roll into open space until it ran smack into the heel of Tony's black rubber soled sneaker. The child stretched out his arms and lunged forward, as Tony said, "Heh, what's this we've got?"

"It's mine," he screamed. "Make him give it back."

Long, brown fingers plucked the toy and swallowed it in a tight grip. Tony, in a fit of perverseness, unravelled the springy cord, letting the wooden ball flip, bounce and gyrate in the whistling air.

"Hush, Kevin," said his mother, powerless to control him, but continuing to hold on to him. "He'll give it back in a second."

"Heh, Man. I didn't know you could do all that." Guillermo tilted his head toward his friend in a mocking half smile.

Tony shrugged. He seemed not to notice that all eyes were on him. Deft, graceful, he let the movements of the yoyo take command, captivated, as were the others, by his own ability.

"Mama, I want it back."

Tony unfolded his body until he stood his full six-foot-three inches and walked over to the child. The little boy saw neither his color nor his height as he held out his small hand.

"It's mine," he said.

Tony squatted beside the chair of the two, the mother and the boy, and flexed his fingers to expose the little red and gold wooden toy that spun magic. No one moved.

"What's your name, Man?"

"Kevin."

"Well, Kevin, thanks for the use of your yoyo."

"It's okay."

Nimble fingers twirled the string one more time before handing it over to the boy.

"Heh, my little brother is even better at this than I am."

Tony snaked a finger into his back jeans pocket and pulled out a wrinkled photograph. Smoothing it out on his knee, he said to Kevin, "His name is Eric."

The two of them huddled over the snapshot.

The minutes hung heavy with quiet. Tina absorbed the fullness, until a single feeling, worldless, sweet and clear lifted from within her. Melange joined in, entwining emotion after emotion in a new sound, building, deepening, rising in the silence. And a new mood, as insistent as a butterfly's winging, caressed the audience. Chelsea knew it was happening, something she wouldn't have dared dream. She saw it in the opening faces. Warmth dripped like molasses over hearts cold with fear as Melange crooned, strumming the still air.

"I know that song," the child piped. "Miss Walker taught us that."

He bounced up and down, a human yoyo, bright with excitement.

"He's got the whole world in His hands." He twisted in her lap. "Right, Mama?"

The mother smiled, including Tony in her warmth. "They teach the little kids that in Sunday school."

"I know."

Chelsea breathed deeply, inhaling the harmony. The baby voice spurted above the A Capella strains, and the shadows retreated. Her anger left, and with it, the fear.

Reminded of the old days—the days of a mother's strength and a grandmother's patience. The unexpected gentleness, like the thaw after a freeze, made her cry. She cried until mascara ran down her face and puddled on the page, blurring the words of her speech. She cried until she started coughing, and her body racked with emotion, started to heave.

And there she stood, a weepy, foolish, unhinged woman, purged by a catastrophe, a human spectacle. She expected a blast of coldness, but nothing but a calm enveloped her. When she could, she quieted. In the miracle of that place, her mother's condemnation transformed into a challenge, a call to something bigger than what she would dream. And with humility, she lifted her eyes and saw an unspoken sympathy in the eyes staring back at her on stage.

Arthur Grahame, raised a steaming cup of coffee in a salute to her. Chelsea smiled. Then she said to her audience,

"You know, the best thing about the arts is that it brings people together."

She didn't remember much after that. She supposed that there had been applause for Melange, and that there had been congratulations for her. She only knew that when she stepped outside on the scalding pavement, she didn't feel the abrasiveness of an August afternoon in Texas.

CONTRIBUTOR'S LIST

nia **akimbo** (Dallas, Texas)

Phyllis W. **Allen** (Fort Worth, Texas)

Cassandra M. **Bailey** (New Orleans, Louisiana)

Bertram **Barnes** (New Orleans, Louisiana)

Gayle **Bell** (Dallas, Texas)

Mawiyah Kai el-Jaman **Bomani** (New Orleans, Louisiana)

Nadir Lasana **Bomani** (New Orleans, Louisiana)

Froswa' **Booker-Drew** (Irving, Texas)

Valerie **Bridgeman-Davis** (Austin, Texas)

sharon **bridgforth** (Austin, Texas)

Emotion **Brown** (aka: Camika Spencer) (Dallas, Texas)

Sybil **Cannon** (Dallas, Texas)

Meta **Carstarphen** (Denton, Texas)

Vicky **Charleston** (Austin, Texas)

Michael Ollie **Clayton** (New Orleans, Louisiana)

Pearl Garrett **Crayton** (Alexandria, Louisiana)

Anthony A. **Douglas** (Fort Worth, Texas)

Freddi Williams **Evans** (New Orleans, Louisiana)

Luvenia **Fears-Porchia** (Bragg Township, Arkansas)

Fred **Fowler** (Fort Worth, Texas)

Monica **Frazier** (Arlington, Texas)

Kaylois **Henry** (Dallas, Texas)

Asabi Olufemi **Ifasola** (Dallas, Texas)

James Thomas **Jackson** (Houston, Texas)

Greg **Johnson** (Fort Worth, Texas)

Glenn **Joshua** (New Orleans, Louisiana)

saddi **khali** (New Orleans, Louisiana)

Bob **Lee** (Houston, Texas)

Ife Nzingha Talibah **Mahdi** (Dallas, Texas)

Michele L. **Majors** (Dallas, Texas)

Jas. **Mardis** (Dallas, Texas)

Charley **Moon** (Dallas, Texas)

Emily M. **Newsome** (Dallas, Texas)

Adrienne **Norris** (Dallas, Texas)

Lindsay **Patterson** (Alexandria, Louisiana, now living in New
York)

Chuck **Perkins** (New Orleans, Louisiana)

Kalamu ya **Salaam** (New Orleans, Louisiana)

Tim **Seibles** (Dallas, Texas, now living in Norfolk, Virginia)

Bernestine **Singley** (Duncanville, Texas)

Ana **Sisnet** (Austin, Texas)

Zenaura Melynia **Smith** (Marrero, Louisiana)

Monica Denise **Spears** (New Orleans, Louisiana)

Clifton L. **Taulbert** (Tulsa, Oklahoma)

Jesse G. **Truvillion** (Big Thicket, Texas, now living in
Jacksonville, Florida)

Von (aka: Kasandra Jones) (Dallas, Texas)

Keith **Walker** (Fort Worth, Texas)

INDEX